I0819464

DRINK ONE
FOR THE TEAM

DRINK ONE FOR THE TEAM

75 Winning Cocktail Recipes Inspired by Legendary Sporting Events

Chris Vola

Illustrations by
Heedayah Lockman

UNION SQUARE & CO.
NEW YORK

Union Square & Co.
Hachette Book Group
1290 Avenue of the Americas, New York, NY 10104
unionsquareandco.com
@unionsqandco

First Edition: May 2026

Union Square & Co. is an imprint of Grand Central Publishing, a division of Hachette Book Group, Inc. The Union Square & Co. name and logo are registered trademarks of Hachette Book Group, Inc.

Union Square & Co. books may be purchased in bulk for business, educational, or promotional use. For information, please contact your local bookseller or the Hachette Book Group Special Markets Department at special.markets@hbgusa.com.

Editors: Caitlin Leffel and Nicole Fisher
Designer: Renée Bollier
Project Editors: Ivy McFadden and Donna Wright
Production Manager: Terence Campo
Copy Editor: Theresa M. Deal

Additional image credits: Shutterstock.com: cover (spine), 14, 26, 36, 48, 54, 64, 74, 86, 96, 104, 110, 122, 132, 142, 154, 191

Library of Congress Control Number has been applied for.

ISBNs: 978-1-4549-6125-3 (hardcover)
978-1-4549-6126-0 (ebook)

Printed in China
1010

10 9 8 7 6 5 4 3 2 1

FOR DAD

CONTENTS

INTRODUCTION

FEW THINGS IN LIFE can match the unmitigated pleasure of attending a live sporting event. From the thrill of real-time action on the field or in the arena to the enthusiasm of a frantic crowd collectively pulsing in the elation or anxiety of every point, goal, or touchdown, it's a uniquely memorable, sensory-heavy experience, one that millions of fans around the world amplify further with the assistance of a frosty beverage (or several).

That's not a new phenomenon: Drinking and sports have gone hand in hand since civilization's earliest days. Ancient Egyptian spectators quenched their thirst at rowing and gymnastics matches with freshly brewed beer, Romans frequently attended gladiatorial battles accompanied by booze-filled flasks, and both competitors and onlookers at the first Greek Olympics liberally fortified themselves—and soothed nagging injuries—with diluted wine by the jugful.

And although you probably won't find many contemporary professional athletes openly imbibing during competitions, watching them play with a tasty drink in hand has been par (or bar) for the course since at least the 1880s, when the American Association, an early professional baseball league run largely by saloon owners and distillers, began promoting the sale of alcoholic beverages during games. Today, beer is as synonymous with America's Pastime as Babe Ruth, whose whiskey-tinged, Prohibition-era exploits were as prodigious as his home run output.

The rise of modern athletics as a worldwide cultural phenomenon also coincided, rather fortuitously, with the Golden Age of Cocktails, an era when the first great drink-slingers were churning out all-time classic libations at an unmatched pace. Several of these liquid delicacies found their way to the grandstands of iconic athletic events, becoming so synonymous with the pageantry and history that it's now impossible to imagine the Kentucky Derby without a mint julep, Wimbledon without a Pimm's Cup, or the Masters without an Azalea Cocktail.

In the current world of twenty-four-hour live streams, surround-sound speakers, and high-definition screens, it's nearly as exciting to enjoy those hallowed spectacles from the comfort of home, mixing up their signature drinks yourself. But why stop there? What about whipping up the perfect game-night tipple for every major global sporting event, regardless of who you and your like-minded guests (or opposing team-loving frenemies) might be rooting for?

Now you can, with *Drink One for the Team*.

As New York Yankees legend Derek Jeter once said, "There may be people that have more talent than you, but there's no excuse for anyone to work harder than you do." With this cocktail playbook in hand, there's no excuse for you not to be an all-star home bartender, regardless of who's playing!

BARWARE AND GLASSWARE

Being prepared and having the proper gear is a must for both world-class athletes and star drink-slingers. The following essential items will give your personal bar setup an unbeatable home-field advantage when hosting game-day watch parties. Or if you decide to take your mixological talents on the road, this equipment will fit nicely into a gym bag.

BARWARE

Barspoons: Barspoons, like athletes, come in a seemingly endless variety of shapes and sizes. But you'll only need two: a thin, long-handled spoon with a teardrop-shaped bowl for stirring—a long chopstick also works great in a pinch—and a sturdier, wider spoon for cracking and shaping ice.

Hawthorne Strainer: Use a Hawthorne strainer for stirred and shaken drinks. This flat-topped favorite of cocktail bartenders has a coiled wire around the edge that fits snugly into any glass or shaker.

Ice Molds: Unless you've got a perma-frozen hockey pond in your backyard, you're going to want to invest in a couple of silicone ice cube molds to create your own big, sexy blocks of ice. To take your cocktail game to the next level, you'll also want ones that form rectangular blocks called Collins spears, which are ideal for tall drinks like the Oklahoma Prairie Fire (page 25).

Jigger: On the court or behind the bar, accuracy is everything. Use a jigger (or jiggers) with 2-ounce, 1½-ounce, 1-ounce, ¾-ounce, and ½-ounce markings. In instances where a drink calls for a ¼-ounce, use your best judgment.

Mixing Glass: Your favorite team's commemorative pint glass will work fine, but if you're looking to splurge on a professional mixing glass, choose a sturdy one that can hold at least 2 cups of ice and booze.

Muddler: Heavy, smooth, plastic muddlers work well and are easy to clean. Avoid wooden muddlers and those with perforated ends. And in the event of a potentially devastating upset, avoid placing muddlers of any variety near your most volatile friends on game day.

Peeler: Any inexpensive Y-shaped peeler will offer more control than a straight vegetable peeler, hopefully keeping your fingers off the disabled list.

Shakers: Professional bartenders usually opt for a Boston shaker set (two metal tumblers of different sizes that fit together) due to their larger capacity and efficiency in high-volume situations. But if you're more of a finesse player, serving up a few carefully crafted sippers from the relative safety of your home bar, it's more than fine to use a classic three-piece shaker (the kind with a built-in strainer).

GLASSWARE

Champagne Flute: A stemmed glass, the champagne flute has a slender, elongated bowl and is used for elegant drinks comprised mostly of champagne and other sparkling wines like those traditionally enjoyed by athletes and/or teams celebrating a championship victory.

Collins Glass/Tall Glass/Tiki Mug: Larger glassware comes in a variety of styles, from simple to wildly ornate. In the cocktail world, the most common of these is a cylindrical tumbler called the Collins glass. For the purposes of this book, that vessel can be used for any tall drink requiring ice and club soda, such as the Bright & Windy (page 139), or tropically inspired concoctions like the Pat Cash Grand Slam Cocktail (page 95) that require lots of crushed ice. However, a standard kitchen water glass or pint glass will work just fine.

Coupe: This classic stemmed glass is used for most drinks served without ice, such as a Southern Hemisphere (page 109) or Pink Lady (page 35), and should have a semicircular bowl that can hold at least 5 fluid ounces. While you might like the look of a V-shaped martini glass—*why?*—it's best to avoid these monstrosities of the Appletini era, as they're generally overly large and sloshy.

Julep Cup: An iconic and enduring symbol of the Kentucky Derby (page 99), the stainless steel or copper julep cup is a descendant of the silver vessels that arose in the American South in the eighteenth and nineteenth centuries. All three metals are great at keeping drinks like the mint julep colder for longer by retaining the temperature of the ice.

Rocks Glass: Also referred to as an Old Fashioned glass or a lowball glass, this short and stout tumbler is used for spirit-forward drinks served on ice, or "on the rocks." Rocks glasses typically hold 6 to 10 fluid ounces.

Double Rocks Glass: This slightly roomier tumbler usually holds 12 to 16 fluid ounces and is ideal for higher-volume stirred drinks as well as any shaken, citrusy cocktail that requires ice, such as the Gordon's Cup (page 57).

Wine Glass: Perfect for fizzy, spritz-style drinks like the Last Whistle (page 61), this household staple, depending on its size, can also be used in place of a coupe, champagne flute, or Collins glass when needed.

SYRUPS

Health-conscious athletes and fitness-savvy fans around the world bemoan the use of sweeteners (despite evidence that small amounts of simple carbohydrates, like sugar, are great for providing a quick burst of energy and improving athletic performance). Nevertheless, sweet elements are crucial for creating perfectly balanced cocktails. The following easy-to-make syrups are used frequently in the drinks in this book.

GINGER SYRUP

YIELD VARIES

1 part superfine sugar
1 part fresh ginger juice (see Note)

Combine the sugar and ginger juice in a nonreactive airtight container and stir until the sugar has completely dissolved. Cover and store in the refrigerator for up to 5 days.

NOTE: *To make ginger juice, simply peel and slice fresh ginger into pieces small enough to fit through the mouth of a juicer, then feed the pieces into the machine.*

POMEGRANATE SYRUP

YIELD VARIES

4 parts simple syrup (see below)
1 part pomegranate juice concentrate, such as FruitFast

Combine the simple syrup and pomegranate juice concentrate in an airtight container and stir until well blended. Cover and store in the refrigerator for up to 1 week.

HONEY SYRUP

YIELD VARIES

1 part water
3 parts honey

In a small saucepan, bring the water to a simmer over medium heat; do not allow it to boil. Combine the honey and hot water in a heat-safe airtight container and stir until well blended. Cover and store in the refrigerator for up to 5 days.

SIMPLE SYRUP

YIELD VARIES

1 part superfine sugar
1 part water

Combine the sugar and water in an airtight container and stir until the sugar has dissolved. Cover and store in the refrigerator for up to 5 days.

NOTE: *To make Demerara syrup, follow the same instructions using Demerara sugar in place of superfine sugar.*

BASEBALL & SOFTBALL

MLB HOME RUN DERBY

Dinger. Jack. Moon shot. Four-bagger. Tater. Blast. Bomb. Home run. Whatever you choose to call it, crushing a baseball out of the park is, unquestionably, one of the sweetest—and some might say, sexiest—moments in all of sports. Immortal sluggers like Babe Ruth, Hank Aaron, and Barry Bonds, while skilled in many facets of the game, are almost exclusively remembered today for their prodigious long balls. And no day features more brutally launched baseballs than the annual Home Run Derby, which, since 1985, has been held every July on the eve of Major League Baseball's All-Star Game.

While the contest's format has varied over the years, the overall concept remains the same: Eight of MLB's most powerful batters trying to out-swing each other during timed, head-to-head, single-elimination duels; whoever hits the most home runs in the final round is crowned champion. All pitches (often thrown by the players' coaches) are delivered much slower than usual, making for some truly memorable performances, like the Seattle Mariners' Julio Rodríguez hitting forty-one home runs in a single round in 2023 or Hall of Famer Ken Griffey Jr. winning an unprecedented third title in 1999.

As majestic as a home run can be, it's also a relatively difficult feat to accomplish in most professional stadiums. One major exception is Denver's Coors Field, home of the Colorado Rockies, whose mile-high altitude causes balls to travel 5 to 10 percent farther than they would at sea level. Colorado is also the home of TINCUP whiskey, which features prominently in the Green Derby from bartender Lucinda Sterling. A play on the classic Brown Derby, its name evokes the verdant hue of a ballfield, while its tangy, citrusy, slightly spicy finish provides the same excitement as watching monstrous athletes send countless baseballs into the stratosphere.

Booze and home runs have gone together for more than a century, back to the days when Babe Ruth would launch bombs while still half in the bag. But perhaps the most impressive tipsy-while-mashing performance goes to two-time Home Run Derby participant Jose Canseco. During a game in the 1990s, Canseco allegedly chugged a beer before his first at-bat and proceeded to hit a monster home run. Before his next plate appearance, he went back into the clubhouse and drank another can, hit another home run, then did the same thing a third time. And while his fourth beer failed to produce another homer, that still sounds like one heck of a happy hour.

GREEN DERBY

MAKES 1 DRINK

- 2 ounces Colorado whiskey, such as TINCUP (bourbon also works well in a pinch)
- ¾ ounce fresh grapefruit juice
- ½ ounce Amber maple syrup
- ½ ounce ginger syrup (see page 13)
- 2 dashes Orinoco bitters, such as The Dead Rabbit Orinoco Bitters

Combine all ingredients in an ice-filled shaker. Shake vigorously for 15 seconds and strain into a coupe.

DARVISH
11

WORLD BASEBALL CLASSIC

Although Major League Baseball has called its annual playoff finale a "World" or "World's" Series for well over a century, the Fall Classic has only ever featured teams from the United States (with the lone exception being the Toronto Blue Jays, back-to-back winners in 1992 and 1993). In the early 2000s, MLB and various international baseball organizations sought to create a truly global tournament modeled after soccer's World Cup, and in 2006, they debuted the World Baseball Classic. Held every four years in early March, it's quickly become one of the most-viewed sporting events (with an average audience nearly three times that of the World Series), and the only world championship that features the best baseball players representing their home countries.

The twenty-team tournament has produced more than a few upsets in its relatively brief history, including some surprisingly deep runs from Cinderella squads like the Netherlands and Israel. But the teams that dominate the tournament tend to come from traditional baseball hot spots like mainland North America, the Caribbean, and, most impressively, Japan, with its unprecedented three titles (as of 2025). That Japanese commitment to excellence is evident both in legendary performances by superstars like Yu Darvish and Shohei Ohtani and in the country's sought-after whisky, which forms the delicate, barley-forward base of the Perfect Game. Containing nine ingredients (matching the innings in a game), this fresh, fruity, and exceptionally boozy tower of tiki also features tropical flavors prevalent in the cuisines of baseball-crazy nations like the Dominican Republic, Cuba, and Venezuela, and will sneak up on you quicker than an inside slider if you don't keep your eye on the ball (or glass).

Attending a Japanese baseball game is a truly unique experience, from the constant organized cheering by supporters of both the home and away teams to the concession stands featuring eel, squid, and sushi instead of hot dogs and Cracker Jacks. One thing American fans will find familiar is a love for mid-game brews, which in Japan are provided by ubiquitous *biiru no uriko*, or beer girls, who pour their wares directly from freshly tapped kegs strapped to their backs.

PERFECT GAME

MAKES 1 DRINK

1½ ounces blended Japanese whisky
1 ounce fresh pineapple juice
½ ounce fresh lime juice
¼ ounce vanilla liqueur
¼ ounce velvet Falernum
¼ ounce cane syrup
2 dashes Angostura bitters
1 barspoon absinthe
Pinch of freshly grated cinnamon
1 sprig mint, for garnish

Combine the whisky, juices, vanilla liqueur, velvet Falernum, cane syrup, bitters, absinthe, and cinnamon in a shaker. Add 1 or 2 ice pebbles, shake for 5 seconds, and pour into a Collins glass or tiki mug. Fill the glass two-thirds of the way with crushed ice. Add a straw and top with more crushed ice. Place the mint sprig on top of the ice.

THE WORLD SERIES

One of the most extraordinary championship events in North American sports, the World Series very nearly died in its infancy. The best-of-seven-games Fall Classic, as it's now known, was conceived in 1903 as a postseason battle for bragging rights between the champions of the two major baseball organizations at the time: the old-money National League (NL) and the upstart American League (AL), which had commenced operations two years prior. When the AL's Boston Red Stockings shocked the world by winning the inaugural series, disgruntled NL team owners refused to participate in future interleague contests, leading to a moratorium on the event the following year. Cooler heads—and the prospect of extra ticket sales—ultimately prevailed, as the series was resumed in 1905 and continues to be the jewel of the baseball calendar, surviving wars, natural disasters, scandals, and player strikes, while showcasing the game's best talent and thrilling, high-pressure moments at the plate and in the field, year after year.

For seven-time World Series champions Babe Ruth and Mickey Mantle, a mixed drink (or several) wasn't just the preferred refreshment after a hard-fought victory, playoffs, or otherwise. It was also the breakfast of champions. The Great Bambino was said to start his day with no less than a quart of whiskey and ginger ale, while The Mick would soothe his frequent hangovers with a White Russian–style concoction made with equal parts brandy, Kahlúa, and cream.

There's an old baseball adage that defense and pitching win championships. Over the decades, otherworldly performances by Hall of Fame hurlers like Sandy Koufax and Mariano Rivera have been crucial to their teams' victories. However, a potent offense is just as vital to success. And nothing can turn the tide faster than a four-run home run, or grand slam, a feat that was only accomplished twenty-two times in the first 120 World Series. A far less rarified—and no less satisfying—Grand Slam also exists in liquid form. A modern adaptation of a heavy-hitting, sugarcane-based classic first described by David A. Embury in *The Fine Art of Mixing Drinks* (1948), this combo of two stylistically divergent yet equally glorious rums, dry curaçao, and pomegranate has enough depth and flavor for an entire seven-game series. If someone offers you one, don't be a stubborn killjoy like an early twentieth-century NL owner and just let it happen.

GRAND SLAM

MAKES 1 DRINK

1 ounce Spanish-style aged rum, such as Flor de Caña 7 Year Gran Reserva rum
1 ounce Goslings Black Seal rum
½ ounce dry curaçao
½ ounce fresh lemon juice
¼ ounce pomegranate syrup (see page 13)
1 orange twist, for garnish

Combine the rums, curaçao, lemon juice, and pomegranate syrup in a shaker. Add 1 or 2 ice pebbles, shake for 5 seconds, and pour into a double rocks glass. Fill the glass two-thirds of the way with crushed ice, add a straw, then top with more ice. Place the orange twist on top of the ice.

LITTLE LEAGUE WORLD SERIES

In an era of nine-figure contracts, multimillion-dollar shoe deals, shady endorsements, and rampant legal sports betting, it's easy for athletes and fans to forget how it was when they were children, playing a game for no other reason than the unbridled joy it brought them. Thankfully, we have the Little League World Series to remind us of those simpler, happy times. Held every summer in South Williamsport, Pennsylvania, the two-week tournament featuring the best ten- to twelve-year-old baseball players in the world is a master class in how pure sports can feel. Beyond the exceptionally high level of play during games—which are free to attend—fans, players, and their families are treated to an unforgettable experience, forging new friendships and soaking in the fun-first atmosphere (and exceptional fried dough from the concession stand). You don't have to be young—just young at heart—to appreciate this magical tradition that longtime MLB manager Terry Francona has described as being "all that is good about baseball."

Despite the Little League World Series' kid-centric vibes, there's plenty of adult fun to be had in the South Williamsport area, where whiskey and moonshine have been produced for centuries. Today, the region is home to more than a dozen highly regarded distilleries and microbreweries, including Fair Play Distillers, whose signature 111-proof bourbon should be of particular interest to lovers of potent brown spirits.

In a rare global event that's all about celebrating childhood passion, where kids are the only stars of the show, there will always be a refreshing innocence inherent to the proceedings. Conversely, when thinking about cocktails and the, shall we say, worldly folks who make them, "innocent" isn't usually the first adjective that comes to mind. The right mocktail, however, can conjure all the carefree childhood vibes, guilt-free. Like the Sandlot Summer: This juicy, gingery blend of unadulterated refreshment is inspired by the classic film *The Sandlot*—required viewing for baseball-obsessed kids in the 1990s—and the fruit-forward soft drinks we'd demolish after long days getting dirty on the infield diamond. Not nearly as sugary as those neon-hued nectars, it's still a charmingly sweet and sour reminder of simpler times.

SANDLOT SUMMER

MAKES 1 DRINK

2 ounces fresh grapefruit juice
¾ ounce ginger syrup (see page 13)
½ ounce fresh lime juice
½ ounce pomegranate syrup (see page 13)
Club soda, to top
1 piece candied ginger, for garnish

Combine the grapefruit juice, ginger syrup, lime juice, and pomegranate syrup in a shaker. Add 1 or 2 ice pebbles, shake for 5 seconds, and pour into an ice-filled Collins glass. Top with club soda. Skewer the piece of candied ginger with toothpicks and perch it on the rim of the glass.

WOMEN'S COLLEGE WORLD SERIES

Every spring, the sixty-four collegiate softball teams that qualify for the NCAA Division I softball tournament share the same goal: make it to Oklahoma City. Since 1990, that's been the site of the Women's College World Series (WCWS), a winner-take-all battle royale of the tournament's last eight surviving teams, contested in double-elimination format, with the final two teams playing in a best-of-three series for the national championship. The close confines at the 13,000-seat Devon Park are wildly electric for every pitch, fueled by the excitement of nail-biting, high-stakes games, and the unbridled enthusiasm of supporters visiting from across the globe. Some fans get to travel much shorter distances than others, like those of the University of Oklahoma Sooners, perpetual attendees of the tournament who play their home games 20 miles away in Norman. From 2000 to 2024, they slugged their way to an unprecedented eight national championships in seventeen WCWS appearances, one of the twenty-first century's most insanely dominant performances in any sport.

Most American professional softball players, particularly members of the storied USA women's national team, passed through Oklahoma City at least once during their collegiate careers. Brush fires also tend to spread across the nearby plains, thanks to the area's mild, semi-arid climate, ideal for games on the diamond but also for potentially incendiary natural events. That blazing heat and smoke can also be found in the Oklahoma Prairie Fire, a darkly intriguing Paloma variant from Ree Drummond. Lip-puckering citrus and pomegranate combine to form a burgundy-orange hue that's a cross between the jersey colors of both the Oklahoma Sooners and the Texas Longhorns, another softball powerhouse. But the drink's uncommonly smooth finish and zesty chili-salt rim will hit the pleasure centers of your brain like a violently slung underhanded fastball, no matter who you're supporting.

If you're running low on time and ingredients but still want to enjoy a beverage during the WCWS, fix yourself an Oklahoma State cocktail. The unofficial drink of both the state and the university, it's a simple combination of vodka, limeade or lemonade, and Sprite, in whatever proportions you deem suitable.

OKLAHOMA PRAIRIE FIRE

MAKES 1 DRINK

Chili-salt, for rimming glass
2 lime wedges
2 ounces mezcal
1 ounce fresh blood orange juice
½ ounce fresh lime juice
½ ounce simple syrup (see page 13)
¼ ounce pomegranate syrup (see page 13)
Club soda, to top

Spread some chili-salt over a small plate. Run 1 lime wedge around the rim of a Collins glass, then dip the rim into the salt to coat. Place a Collins spear or cracked ice in the glass and set aside. Combine the mezcal, blood orange juice, lime juice, simple syrup, and pomegranate syrup in a shaker. Add 1 or 2 ice pebbles, shake for 5 seconds, and pour into the glass. Top with club soda. Place the remaining lime wedge on the rim of the glass.

BASKETBALL

NBA FINALS

In 2014, when listing his "Mount Rushmore" of all-time basketball greats, LeBron James famously left off Bill Russell, who won eleven National Basketball Association (NBA) championships in a thirteen-season career. Asked to respond to the snubbing, the Boston Celtics Hall of Famer smiled and said, "I'm glad [he] did. Basketball is a team game; it's not for individual honors." Since the first NBA Finals tipped off in 1947, that selfless mentality has been crucial to achieving immortality in basketball's biggest best-of-seven-game series. And while some of the sport's most GOATed superstars like James, Michael Jordan, and Shaquille O'Neal have all hoisted the Larry O'Brien Championship Trophy multiple times, they'd never have gotten anywhere near it without exceptional supporting casts. The emphasis on harmonious teamwork, coupled with an always-electric, high-stakes atmosphere, has made the Finals one of the hottest tickets in sports for well over half a century. And with the recent increase in parity in the NBA, as well as a massive infusion of international talent, it looks like things are only going to get spicier.

Reaching the NBA Finals marks the culmination of eight months' worth of blood, sweat, and tears. Starting in October, players need not only the skill and stamina to grind out a grueling eighty-two-game regular season, but also the fortitude to survive an additional three rounds of playoffs to make it to early June and the chance for ultimate glory. That otherwise pleasant time of year inspires both basketball dreams and some exceptionally appetizing seasonal cocktails like Raymond Delaney's Bring June Flowers, which was created at New York's The Up & Up. Wildly fresh, floral, vegetal, and bitter, it's smoother than a Kobe Bryant jump shot, more complex than a Phil Jackson offense, and revitalizing enough to make you feel like a winner, regardless of your favorite team's performance.

NBA Finals winners tend to waste no time celebrating their achievement with beer, champagne, seltzers, and other adult beverages in the locker room. And for party-inclined ballers, that's only the beginning of a well-earned, several-day bender that's been known to decimate those of a lesser tolerance. Like the Denver Nuggets' Bruce Brown, who, after the team's 2023 Finals victory, tried to go drink-for-drink with his 284-pound teammate Nikola Jokić, which left him brutally hungover in a Las Vegas hotel room, where he tweeted: "I want everyone to know, this is Nikola Jokić's fault, that I'm down this bad. I don't know what he had me drinking last night, but I blame it on #15."

BRING JUNE FLOWERS

MAKES 1 DRINK

1½ ounces vodka
½ ounce Suze, or comparable gentian liqueur
¾ ounce fresh lemon juice
¾ ounce jasmine syrup, such as Monin Honey Jasmine Syrup
5 thin cucumber slices

Combine the vodka, Suze, lemon juice, jasmine syrup, and 3 cucumber slices in a shaker. Muddle the cucumber slices, then dump the entire contents of the shaker into a double rocks glass. Fill the glass two-thirds of the way with crushed ice, add a straw, then top with more crushed ice. Perch the remaining 2 cucumber slices on the rim of the glass beside the ice.

WNBA FINALS

Diana Taurasi. Tamika Catchings. Cynthia Cooper. Maya Moore. Lisa Leslie. Arguably the top five WNBA players since the league's founding in 1997, they all have one thing in common: Each has won at least one WNBA Finals and, in doing so, been named Finals MVP, the crown jewel(s) in their already impressive legacies. Simply getting a chance to play in the league's best-of-five championship series is a massive achievement. The women's basketball landscape is increasingly competitive, given the WNBA's relatively short history and small number of teams, as well as the emergence of some truly formidable dynasties. Like the now-dissolved Houston Comets, who, led by Hall-of-Famer Cynthia Cooper-Dyke, won the league's first four titles from 1997 to 2000. Or the superb Minnesota Lynx squads of the 2010s, who captured four championships while appearing in the Finals six times in seven years.

With the league growing from twelve to fifteen franchises in 2026, in addition to an expanded playoff format, it's becoming increasingly difficult to reach the WNBA Finals. But teams looking to experience the rarest heights of women's basketball success still need to possess the same time-tested qualities—star power, chemistry, and a killer instinct on the court. While its name might not conjure aggressive emotions or game-time togetherness, the Tijuana Lady is one tough cocktail. Created by Michael Madrusan at trailblazing West Village neo-speakeasy Little Branch, this female-inspired, tequila-based sipper marries vegetal agave, vanilla-heavy aromatics, and notes of citrus and mango for a finish that's easier than a wide-open layup. Quite welcoming to the senses, it's still best to take this one in stride, as its multi-alcohol combo can, like a three-point-shooting sniper, catch opposing defenses (i.e., careless drinkers) woefully unawares.

In 2024, the Las Vegas Aces, winners of back-to-back WNBA championships in 2022 and 2023, became the first WNBA team to enter into a multiyear partnership with a spirits company, Dos Caras Tequila. Woman-owned and family-operated, Dos Caras is made with 100-percent Blue Weber agave and sustainably produced in Arandas, Jalisco, Mexico, using clean, renewable energy.

TIJUANA LADY

MAKES 1 DRINK

- 1½ ounces tequila, such as Dos Caras Blanco
- 1 ounce Licor 43
- ¾ ounce fresh lime juice
- 2 dashes Angostura bitters
- 1 lime wedge, for garnish

Combine the tequila, Licor 43, lime juice, and bitters in an ice-filled shaker. Shake vigorously for 15 seconds and strain into a coupe. Perch the lime wedge on the rim of the glass.

NCAA MEN'S FINAL FOUR

The biggest daily worries for most college kids consist of whether they've remembered to do their homework and finding out when the cafeteria opens for mac and cheese night. For the lucky few student athletes competing in the NCAA Final Four, the concerns are a bit loftier. Namely: how to achieve basketball immortality.

The last two rounds of the sixty-eight-team, single-elimination NCAA Tournament—appropriately referred to as March Madness and held annually since 1939—represent the climactic conclusion to one of the most thrilling and unpredictable sporting events in the world, a monthlong soap opera on the hardwood for the best college ballers in the U.S., where anything can happen, and often does. With frequent dramatic upsets, shocking Cinderella runs from unheralded underdogs, buzzer-beating shots, insanely passionate student sections, and epic calls from cherished announcers, it's easy to see why, for millions of basketball junkies, casual fans, and sports bettors, March truly is the most wonderful time of the year. And an even more marvelous—and incredibly stressful—joyride for the last four teams left standing.

There are plenty of opportunities for booze-induced good times in and around the grounds of the Final Four, though to get access to what many in college basketball consider the party of the year, you're going to need an invite. Hosted annually on the Sunday of Final Four weekend by eternally jovial announcer Bill Raftery—whose nickname, "Uncle One More," alludes to his marathon-like drinking exploits—the impromptu, all-night dinner is a who's who of fellow media personalities, coaches, former players, and, occasionally, random people whom Raftery met that day. It's considered a great honor to attend, and even more impressive to remain upright and conscious until last call.

The number 6 has been worn by many old-school basketball icons, like Bill Russell and Patrick Ewing, who dominated Final Fours in the days when the NCAA allowed fewer teams into the tournament. In the modern, expanded era, that digit is still of the utmost importance to teams with Final Four aspirations, as it's the number of games most need to win to capture the national championship. It's also prominent in the name of the Six Figure, a bright, smoky, and vegetal Negroni-esque nightcap from Dan Greenbaum. Containing just three ingredients, one assumes the drink's moniker comes from the fact that one whiff of its sumptuous, smartly layered, and subtly honeyed nose is enough to make mezcal lovers feel like at least half a million bucks—which, now that college players are allowed to profit from their name, image, and likeness, is an amount familiar to the game's most visible stars.

SIX FIGURE

MAKES 1 DRINK

1½ ounces mezcal
1¼ ounces white vermouth
¼ ounce yellow Chartreuse
1 lemon twist, for garnish

Combine the mezcal, vermouth, and Chartreuse in a double rocks glass. Add ice and stir with a long-handled spoon for 5 or 6 seconds. Rub the lemon twist around the rim of the glass, peel side down, then place it in the glass.

NCAA WOMEN'S FINAL FOUR

When asked to give a reason for his team's success in the women's NCAA basketball tournament, the University of Connecticut Huskies' Geno Auriemma, the sport's winningest coach and a twelve-time national champion over a thirty-year span, replied: "We win because we get the best players." A clearly oversimplified, tongue-in-cheek statement that still speaks to a universal sports truth, that the teams with the most talent tend not to lose very often.

Since its founding in 1982, the tournament—and particularly its final two rounds—have seen some prodigious stockpiles of superstars from dynastic programs like the University of Tennessee Lady Volunteers, Stanford University Cardinals, and Connecticut, which made the Final Four every season from 2008 to 2022. But recently, as women's college basketball continues to surge in popularity thanks to the dazzling play of transcendent cultural figures like Caitlin Clark and Angel Reese, more teams have joined the ranks of the elite, creating a level of unprecedented excitement, to the point where the 2024 women's Final Four had higher ratings than the men's.

Increased visibility, as well as the opportunity to profit from their names, images, and likenesses, has turned many social-media-savvy college ballers into global fashion icons. But don't get it twisted, once they step onto the court, these finely tuned athletes are all about the business of getting buckets. A trait that's reminiscent of the Pink Lady, a Prohibition-era classic that was, rather misogynistically, thought of as being only for mild-mannered, high-society damsels. Yet, as Jack Townsend writes in *The Bartender's Book* (1951), the bodacious blend of gin, brandy, citrus, grenadine, and egg white "packs a serious wallop" underneath its rosy, playfully frothy facade (that recalls the color of the jerseys teams frequently wear to promote breast cancer awareness). A serious drink for serious bucket-getters.

The University of Iowa's Caitlin Clark, the NCAA's all-time leading scorer and No. 1 2024 WNBA draft pick, had one of the greatest college basketball careers, with the one knock being that she never was able to win a national championship. In 2024, after losing in the Final Four to LSU, she did the next best thing—she took her teammates to Happiest Hour, a random dive bar in Dallas, and treated them to a night of sorrow drowning and team bonding.

PINK LADY

MAKES 1 DRINK

1½ ounces London dry gin, such as Beefeater
¾ ounce fresh lemon juice
¾ ounce pomegranate syrup (see page 13)
½ ounce Laird's Applejack
1 egg white
2 brandy cherries, for garnish

Combine the gin, lemon juice, pomegranate syrup, applejack, and egg white in a shaker. Briefly shake without ice (to emulsify the egg white) for 5 seconds, then add ice and shake vigorously for 15 seconds. Strain into a coupe. Skewer the brandy cherries with a toothpick and perch them on the rim of the glass.

FOOTBALL

NFL DRAFT

Scouts, coaches, and general managers spend countless hours planning for it. Bookies take bets on the outcome months in advance. It's televised on multiple national networks. Sounds like a big game, right? The NFL Draft isn't an on-the-field event, but nonetheless, it's still a major competition. Since 1936, it's been the most common way to recruit new players into the league, with teams drafting in reverse order of their records in the previous season (the team in last place picks first, and the Super Bowl winner picks last). For those doing the selecting, it's a chaotic time, filled with endless strategy and analytics meetings, behind-the-scenes jostling, and last-minute trades to improve draft order. For fans, it's pure prime-time drama, rife with cautious optimism and speculation about which college superstar will make the biggest impact for their new team, both immediately and in the future. Because for long-suffering supporters of some endlessly snakebit franchises (looking at you, New York Jets), the future is usually all they've got.

Held in various NFL cities, the draft is attended by hundreds of diehards who queue for hours to score first-come-first-served tickets, and who wear their emotions on their sleeves—or replica jerseys—while unabashedly praising or critiquing their teams' selections. The same can be said for those watching in their living rooms, where screens destroyed by angrily flung remotes are a common sight. Whether toasting to your squad's imminent success or reevaluating your choices in fandom, the Draft Day cocktail from Michael McCollum is a can't-miss companion. First served at Attaboy Nashville in 2018, the spirit-forward hodgepodge is reminiscent of a Boulevardier but fruitier and less bitter, with an interestingly herbaceous and aniseed-tinged finish and plenty of rum-based funk. Each disparate flavor, like a winning teammate, does exactly the right job in this unquestionable number one pick.

A 2023 study found that the average Green Bay Packers fan consumes 6.3 beers while attending a game, the most of any NFL fan base by a significant margin. It makes perfect sense, then, that Green Bay's craft breweries teamed up to create a special collaborative beer—8th Round Downtown Pale Ale—to serve as an official beverage when the city hosted the 2025 Draft.

DRAFT DAY

MAKES 1 DRINK

1½ ounces rye
½ ounce Smith & Cross Jamaica Rum
½ ounce Gran Classico
½ ounce banana liqueur, such as Giffard Banane du Brésil
1 dash absinthe
1 orange twist, for garnish

Combine the rye, rum, Gran Classico, banana liqueur, and absinthe in a double rocks glass. Add ice and stir with a long-handled spoon for 5 or 6 seconds. Place the orange twist in the glass alongside the ice.

ARMY–NAVY GAME

Cooperation among different military branches is essential to a country's success on the battlefield. On the football field, however, it's an entirely different story. Few collegiate rivalries are older, fiercer, and higher profile than the yearly interservice clash between the Army Black Knights of the United States Military Academy and the Navy Midshipmen of the United States Naval Academy. For more than 120 years, the game—played at a neutral site on the second Saturday of December—has represented far more than just potential bragging rights for the two oldest officer commissioning schools in the United States.

This globally broadcasted, pomp-laden spectacle is attended by presidents, celebrities, and thousands of the academies' alumni and current students, whose traditional pranks, songs, and cheers of "Beat Army!" and "Beat Navy!" are deeply integral to the competitive identities of the respective institutions, as well as the services they represent. And though the game's importance to the overall college football picture has greatly diminished since the middle of the twentieth century, when both programs regularly competed for national championships, it's still a must-watch, uniquely rowdy display of patriotism and school spirit.

The first matchup between the teams occurred on November 29, 1890 (a 24–0 Navy victory), but the most famous cocktail celebrating the rivalry has a much less certain origin. Emerging in the early 1900s and eventually appearing in the pages of David A. Embury's *The Fine Art of Mixing Drinks* (1948), the Army & Navy, a proto-tiki gin sour riff using almond-based orgeat as its sweetener, was popularized at—where else—Washington, DC's Army and Navy Club, a members-only officers' watering hole where it still appears on the menu. Embury famously called the original recipe "horrible," but later versions that balance the drink by toning down the orgeat and adding aromatic bitters are delightful—a treat for both militant-minded mixologists and civilian cocktail newbies.

The Army and Navy Club, which describes itself as a "prestigious home away from home for the most illustrious names in America's military and political history," was also the scene of one of the most important moments in American cocktail history. Namely, it's where the first daiquiri was served on U.S. soil, at one of the club's bars that's now appropriately known as the Daiquiri Lounge.

ARMY & NAVY

MAKES 1 DRINK

2 ounces gin
¾ ounce fresh lemon juice
¾ ounce orgeat
2 dashes Angostura bitters

Combine all ingredients in an ice-filled shaker. Shake vigorously for 15 seconds and strain into a coupe.

COLLEGE FOOTBALL NATIONAL CHAMPIONSHIP

Ironically, for a sport with such a long history and so steeped in tradition as American college football, its most popular and important game has only existed for a fraction of that history. Before the first National Championship bout between the country's two top-ranked programs after the conclusion of the 1998 regular season, the national champion had been determined by journalists, polling committees, and, later, computer algorithms, often leaving incredible—and some would say, more deserving—teams frustrated and without any hardware to show for their efforts. Now, however, more schools can legitimately battle for the Championship Trophy, thanks to the creation of the College Football Playoff in 2014. Originally a Final Four–type situation that expanded to twelve teams in 2024, this much fairer system allows for more drama, more upsets, and way more football. And who can argue with that?

Since its debut, the National Championship has been a literal stomping ground for the best programs in modern history, like the University of Alabama, Ohio State, and LSU, as well as for the best athletes, including several winners of the Heisman Trophy. Given each year to the top performer in college football since 1935, the iconic award depicts a ball-carrier rushing down the field, his free arm stiffly outstretched, and was apparently modeled after New York University running back Ed Smith. Though it's not inspired by the trophy, the football-themed Gold Rusher cocktail from San Francisco bartender Helen Diaz also invokes the image of a seemingly supernatural player plowing through the defense on his way to the end zone. More important, with just one sip, this rich, botanically powerful combination of bourbon, Fernet-Branca, ginger, honey, and lemon will make you feel like a winner, even if your betting app history might suggest otherwise.

The NCAA has always had a dicey relationship with alcohol companies, especially given that many of its student athletes are under the legal drinking age. That's changing now that players can ink name, image, and likeness (NIL) deals with whomever they choose (depending on individual state laws). In 2021, then twenty-three-year-old N'Kosi Perry, quarterback at Florida Atlantic University, signed the first-ever NIL deal to promote a beer/liquor organization, Islamorada Beverages, paving the way for many such deals in the future.

GOLD RUSHER

MAKES 1 DRINK

1½ ounces bourbon
¾ ounce fresh lemon juice
½ ounce Fernet-Branca
½ ounce ginger syrup (see page 13)
½ ounce honey syrup (see page 13)
1 sprig mint, for garnish

Combine the bourbon, lemon juice, Fernet-Branca, ginger syrup, and honey syrup in an ice-filled shaker. Shake vigorously for 15 seconds and strain over ice into a double rocks glass. Place the mint sprig in the glass beside the ice.

50

SUPER BOWL

National Football League superstar and longtime announcer Terry Bradshaw perfectly summed up the magnitude of his sport's ultimate game: "As a player, it says everything about you if you made the Hall of Fame. But, then again, boy . . . there's something about winning a Super Bowl."

Originally called the AFL-NFL World Championship Game (before the rival American Football League merged with the NFL in 1970), the first edition of "Football's Favorite Sunday" took place on January 15, 1967, in Los Angeles, with the Green Bay Packers defeating the Kansas City Chiefs by a score of 35–10. Since then, the Super Bowl has evolved into a massive cultural phenomenon. America's most treasured unofficial holiday, it's an explosive show of gridiron prowess, music, and pyrotechnics that transcends athletics, where the halftime show can be a more interesting conversation piece than the game itself. Franchises and players lucky enough to experience the confetti-covered thrill of victory earn themselves a one-way ticket to instant immortality, while defeat has the opposite effect, erasing otherwise great teams and replacing their wins with the knowledge that they couldn't crack it on the brightest stage. As iconic football personality John Madden once put it, "That's the biggest gap in sports, the difference between the winner and the loser of the Super Bowl."

If you want the signature drink at your next Super Bowl party to be as memorable as a game-clinching touchdown, you've got to whip up a communal libation with equal parts potency and exquisite flavor. In a nutshell, that's the Super Sunday Punch from Chicago bartender Mike Ryan. Featuring two of the country's oldest and most venerated spirits, bourbon and Laird's Applejack, it's a beautiful blitz of Americana, highlighted by ruby red grapefruit juice, sweet tea, honey, and enough spice to entice the most unsportsmanlike of palates. Just make sure your guests get home safely, as several will inevitably end up groggier than a quarterback that's been sacked a few too many times.

Regardless of who's playing, fans of every NFL franchise religiously tune in to the Super Bowl, with mountains of beverages and snacks at the ready. A 2025 survey of eating and drinking habits conducted by sports betting website nj.bet concluded that the Baltimore Ravens fan base spends the most money on alcohol for the big game (at around $29 per person), while the typical barbecue-loving Houston Texan fan consumes a gut-busting 3,548 calories during the festivities, the largest amount by a significant margin.

SUPER SUNDAY PUNCH

SERVES APPROXIMATELY 25

25 whole cloves
6 cinnamon sticks
1 teaspoon whole allspice
1 (750 mL) bottle 100-proof bourbon
1 (750 mL) bottle Laird's Applejack
25 ounces fresh ruby red grapefruit juice
25 ounces honey
10 ounces sweet tea
1 apple, cored and sliced, for garnish

Wrap the cloves, cinnamon sticks, and allspice in cheesecloth, tie into a bundle, and place in a punch bowl. Add the bourbon, Applejack, grapefruit juice, honey, and sweet tea and stir thoroughly with a long-handled spoon. Fill the punch bowl with large ice cubes and briefly stir again. Place the apple slices in the punch bowl. Serve in punch cups.

GREY CUP

Myopic Americans might have you believe that the Super Bowl is the only prime-time pro football championship worth watching. Take a trip up north to the frosty Canadian gridiron and you'll quickly learn that's not the case. The Grey Cup, the final game of the Canadian Football League (CFL) season—and the name of the trophy that's given to the winning team—is Canada's biggest sporting event, drawing about 4 million television viewers annually. Predating the formation of the CFL by decades, the Cup was commissioned in 1909 and was originally a contest between both amateur and professional clubs before the current east-versus-west, all-pro format was established in the 1920s. Unlike its south-of-the-border counterpart, the game is played in late fall, primarily in outdoor stadiums, and frequently in wildly inclement weather. Like 1950's "Mud Bowl," in which Winnipeg Blue Bombers linebacker Buddy Tinsley nearly drowned in a puddle of sludge. Or 1977's "Ice Bowl," where the Astroturf at Montreal's Olympic Stadium completely froze over, causing the field to resemble a hockey rink. Doesn't get much more exciting (or more "Canada") than that.

Over the decades, the Toronto Argonauts have weathered mud, ice, fog, snow, and just about everything else Mother Nature doles out to become the most successful Canadian football team, with nineteen Grey Cup titles as of this writing. But to survive off the field, it's best to look to the home province of the rival Montreal Alouettes, where there's a cocktail that's won more battles against cold weather than any other. The Caribou, a potent, warming, and rejuvenating mixture of whisky, red wine, and maple syrup, has been a wintertime pick-me-up for Quebec's drinkers since colonial times. And the best part is you don't have to be a Canadian (or already half-frozen) to try one for yourself.

The CFL's most die-hard fans are known as an especially rowdy, beverage-loving bunch, none more famous than Ottawa Redblacks season ticket holder Rick Lemay, also known as Mr. Shoe Beer. During the third quarter of every home game, Lemay fires up the crowds at TD Place Stadium by—you guessed it—pouring a tallboy into one of his shoes and chugging it, delighting fellow Canadian football freaks and terrifying germophobes and podiatrists everywhere.

CARIBOU

MAKES 1 DRINK

2 ounces Canadian whisky or rye whiskey
1 ounce red wine
¼ ounce Amber maple syrup
1 sprig rosemary, for garnish

Combine the whisky, red wine, and maple syrup in an ice-filled mixing glass. Stir with a long-handled spoon for 25 to 30 seconds and strain into a coupe. Place the rosemary sprig in the glass.

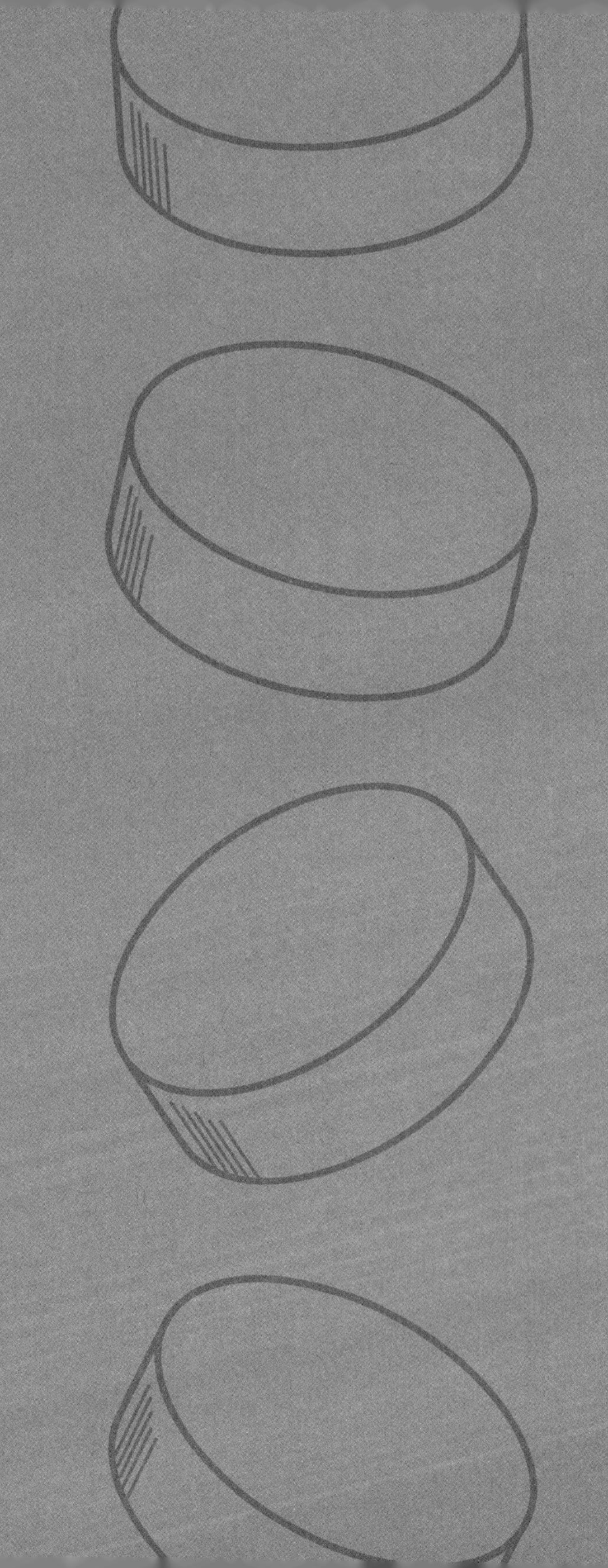

HOCKEY

STANLEY CUP FINALS

From after-work beer leagues to upper-echelon athletics, just about every team sports competition involves some kind of trophy. In North America, none is older or more famous than the Stanley Cup, which has been presented annually to the winner of the NHL playoffs since 1926. Commissioned in 1892 by avid hockey fan Lord Frederick Stanley, then the Governor General of Canada, the large silver bowl—which would later be affixed to a cylindrical base where the names of championship teams and players are still inscribed—was originally called the Dominion Challenge Cup and was presented to the best amateur hockey club in Canada, as determined by league record and challenge games, until 1909, when Canadian and American professional teams began to exclusively compete for it.

Unlike in other major sports, the team that wins the Stanley Cup Finals gets access to the Cup for one hundred days, with every player and staff member getting a day with it however they like. The tradition has, unsurprisingly, led to epic (and often booze-fueled) shenanigans, including untold gallons of champagne being consumed directly from the Cup's bowl. The trophy has also been kicked across a frozen canal, dropped into a bonfire, used as a dog food receptacle and geranium planter, and taken on roller-coaster rides and fishing trips. Perhaps its most egregious treatment occurred in 1940 at the hands of the then-defending-champion New York Rangers. To celebrate paying off the mortgage on Madison Square Garden, team management burned the mortgage documents in the Cup. When the fire got out of control, several Rangers players allegedly urinated on the trophy, leading to the Curse of 1940, which purportedly lasted until the team finally won another Stanley Cup Finals in 1994.

While the Rangers and seventeen other American teams have hoisted the Cup at least once, the trophy has spent far more time in its native Canada, with the Montreal Canadiens boasting the most Finals victories at twenty-four. It makes sense then that any drink celebrating hockey's biggest prize should include Canada's proudest native spirit, rye whisky, as well as a healthy dose of champagne. The Lord Stanley 93—which comes in a Cup-like coupe glass—checks both boxes, while also featuring maple syrup and applejack, the oldest distilled spirit in the United States, for a delightfully bubbly, citrusy, and fruity concoction that's perfect for toasting any Finals-bound team.

According to "Keeper of the Cup" Phil Pritchard, curator of the Hockey Hall of Fame, the Stanley Cup can hold up to fourteen cans of beer, something he's learned firsthand after attending countless postseason festivities in his official role as the trophy's chaperone.

LORD STANLEY 93

MAKES 1 DRINK

½ ounce Canadian rye whisky
½ ounce Laird's Applejack
½ ounce fresh lemon juice
½ ounce Amber maple syrup
2 dashes Angostura bitters
Champagne, to top
1 lemon twist, for garnish

Combine the rye, applejack, lemon juice, maple syrup, and bitters in an ice-filled shaker. Shake vigorously for 15 seconds and strain into a coupe. Top with champagne. Rub the lemon twist around the rim of the glass, peel side down, then place it in the glass.

NCAA FROZEN FOUR

March (and April) Madness doesn't just take place on the hardwood. Like its basketball counterpart, the NCAA Division I hockey tournament is a springtime, single-elimination showdown of its sport's brightest collegiate stars, culminating in a final weekend of gritty, dramatic semifinals and championship action known as the Frozen Four. First held in 1948—a decisive victory for the powerhouse Michigan Wolverines—the tournament has served as the biggest platform for the best up-and-coming American and international talent, and has played host to countless memorable moments, abnormally high-scoring games, historic individual performances, and excitingly improbable comebacks. It's also unique in the world of college athletics in that many perennially contending schools, such as Minnesota Duluth and Lake Superior State, primarily compete at the lower Division II or Division III levels in other sports.

Hockey players of all ages and abilities, whether vying for a national championship or trying to dominate the neighborhood pond, take special pride in achieving a hat trick, or scoring three goals in a single game. The Frozen Four has had no shortage of such performances, including University of Maine's Jim Montgomery, who accomplished the feat in a mere four minutes and thirty-five seconds during the 1993 title game. That's more time than you'll need to stir up a Hat Trick cocktail, a sugarcane-based Manhattan (or martini) variation that, as its name suggests, contains three ingredients in equal proportions—dark rum, white rum, and sweet vermouth. When combined, dark rum's inherent richness melds effortlessly with the crisper notes of white rum and the sweet complexity of the fortified Italian wine. Smooth and supple, its finish is as graceful as an offensive-minded hockey savant weaving through opposing defenses and turning the back of the net into a puck graveyard.

College hockey fans take part in some crazy traditions, like at the University of New Hampshire, where they throw a large frozen fish onto the ice after their team's first goal. Or North Dakota State, which puts on a techno concert between the second and third periods of every game, complete with a light show. Another particularly enthusiastic celebration occurs at the University of Wisconsin, where, after a goal, the entire student section erupts into a song and dance act fueled by a rendition of The Champs' classic hit song "Tequila"—and, most likely, more than a few shots of that eponymous liquor.

HAT TRICK

MAKES 1 DRINK

1 ounce dark rum
1 ounce white rum
1 ounce sweet vermouth

Combine all ingredients in an ice-filled mixing glass. Stir with a long-handled spoon for 25 to 30 seconds and strain into a coupe.

SOCCER

FIFA WORLD CUP

Many sports have international tournaments that are described as "world cups." But when someone mentions *The* World Cup, everyone knows what they're talking about. Soccer's hallowed quadrennial clash of forty-eight countries' national teams—the most popular sporting event on the planet, by far—lights up millions of TV sets from the High Arctic to the deepest jungles, transcending borders and bringing together billions of football-obsessed crazies for a monthlong celebration of the beautiful game. Founded by soccer's governing body, the Fédération Internationale de Football Association (FIFA), in 1930, the inaugural Cup was hosted—and won—by Uruguay, the first of many dominant performances by South American nations. And while teams from that continent and Europe are the only squads to hoist the FIFA World Cup Trophy as of 2026, fans everywhere continue tuning in for inspiring stories of underdog triumphs, heart-stopping penalty kicks, unmatched displays of national pride, and unforgettable moments that become etched in humanity's collective memory, fostering a sense of universal solidarity that's second to none.

Association football as we know it today originated in the nineteenth century on the ballfields of England, whose national team reached the pinnacle of sporting success with its 4–2 drubbing of West Germany in the 1966 World Cup (and has taken no small amount of razzing from its international rivals for its inability to replicate that feat). It's also a country whose cocktail culture is as impressive as its soccer prowess, especially when it comes to gin, its celebrated local spirit. One of the best ways to enjoy that botanically blessed liquor is in a Gordon's Cup, a modern classic from legendary cocktail pioneer Sasha Petraske. Beautifully light and savory, chock-full of lime and cucumber goodness, this muddled masterpiece is partially inspired by the Caipirinha, the national beverage of fellow soccer dynamo Brazil. While the World Cup captures the hearts of soccer fans around the globe, this Cup is guaranteed to win over their taste buds, one sip at a time.

The cost of achieving a decent buzz during a game can fluctuate greatly, depending on where you're watching. Historically, no sporting event has put a bigger hurt on boozehounds' wallets than the 2022 World Cup in Doha, Qatar. Fans looking to score drinks at stadiums in the predominantly Muslim country had to first purchase "corporate hospitality" tickets, with prices starting at a (literally) sobering $22,000.

GORDON'S CUP

MAKES 1 DRINK

2 ounces gin
¾ ounce simple syrup (see page 13)
5 thin cucumber slices
4 lime wedges
Pinch of salt, for garnish
Pinch of black pepper, for garnish

Combine the gin, simple syrup, 3 cucumber slices, and lime wedges in a shaker. Muddle thoroughly and fill the shaker with cracked ice. Shake for 5 or 6 seconds and pour the contents of the shaker into a double rocks glass. Place the remaining 2 cucumber slices in the glass beside the ice. Sprinkle with the salt and pepper.

FIFA WOMEN'S WORLD CUP

Anyone who can even remotely recall the pop culture landscape of 1999 remembers Brandi Chastain. Specifically, an image of the United States women's national soccer team defender, seconds after scoring a game-winning penalty shoot-out goal against China in the 1999 FIFA Women's World Cup final and removing her jersey, fists raised and mouth agape in a moment of pure, unfiltered joy. Considered somewhat controversial at the time, Chastain's sports-bra-exposing celebration became an inspiring symbol for women's athletics worldwide and a great example of the passion the World Cup instills in participating players. That infectious intensity has been witnessed by exponentially more eyes since China hosted the inaugural Cup in 1991; today it's the most popular women's sporting event in the world, and, with approximately 2 billion viewers, one of the most watched competitions—male or female—in the years that it's played.

Twenty years after the infamous Chastain incident, the American team once again invited controversy at the 2019 World Cup. After scoring a game-winning goal against England, U.S. cocaptain Alex Morgan raised her fingers to her mouth, mimicking the act of drinking a cup of tea—100 million of which are consumed by the British every day. The gesture upset some critics who felt it was not only a jibe against the English team, but an aggression-inspiring reference to the Boston Tea Party of 1773, which kick-started the American Revolution.

The inherent patriotic fervor surrounding the Women's World Cup means that championship squads receive some seriously regal treatment upon returning to their home countries. That's particularly true of the United States national team, winners of four of the first nine editions of the tournament, whose players are recognizable to more fans than their counterparts on the men's team. Conquerors of the Cup deserve all the accolades, as well as an appropriately royal libation to toast their success. Like the Queen Bee, which was first described in Charles H. Baker Jr.'s 1951 travelogue, *The South American Gentleman's Companion*. An apple brandy sour embellished with honey and curaçao, it's a rich, aromatic, and slightly sweet ode to collective greatness, finishing with a lemony tang that's zestier than the fiercest international rivalries.

QUEEN BEE

MAKES 1 DRINK

2 ounces apple brandy
¾ ounce fresh lemon juice
½ ounce dry curaçao
½ ounce honey syrup (see page 13)
1 orange twist, for garnish

Combine the apple brandy, lemon juice, dry curaçao, and honey syrup in an ice-filled shaker. Shake vigorously for 15 seconds and strain into a coupe. Rub the orange twist around the rim of the glass, peel side down, then place it in the glass.

Regardless of who you're supporting in the Champions League Final, the folks at *Drinking Dojo Blog* have created a drinking game that's a great way to (responsibly) enjoy the camaraderie of friends during the match.

GAME RULES

1. **Kickoff Cheers**
   As soon as the match begins, everyone raises their glass for a kickoff cheers. Take a sip to start the game.

2. **Goal Celebration**
   Whenever a team scores a goal, everyone must take a drink. Bonus sip if it's a header or a goal from outside the penalty box.

3. **Foul Play**
   If a yellow card is issued, take a sip. If a red card is issued, finish your drink.

4. **Penalty Tension**
   When a penalty is awarded, everyone takes a sip. If the penalty results in a goal, take an additional sip.

5. **Corner Kicks**
   Every corner kick means a sip for everyone. If a goal is scored directly from a corner, finish your drink.

6. **Commentator Clichés**
   Whenever the commentator uses phrases like "end-to-end stuff" or "it's a game of two halves," take a sip.

7. **Player Substitutions**
   Each substitution calls for a quick sip. If your favorite player is subbed in, take an extra sip.

8. **Extra Time Excitement**
   If the match goes into extra time, everyone takes a sip at the start. Brace yourselves with another sip before the penalty shoot-out.

UEFA CHAMPIONS LEAGUE FINAL

As dominant as Europe's national soccer teams have been in global competitions, the continent's domestic clubs are even more impressive. Winning any of the top European leagues—widely considered the best in the world—is a massive accomplishment, but the most elite teams have their eyes on an even bigger prize: the Champions League title. The sport's most prestigious annual club competition, organized by the fifty-five-country Union of European Football Associations (UEFA), the Champions League is a round-robin tournament of national league champions (with the five highest-ranked leagues providing four teams each), culminating in the UEFA Champions League Final. The ultimate continental showdown, first won by Real Madrid in 1956, it's a dramatic confluence of tactical brilliance, individual mastery, and sheer quality, where unforgettable moments are etched into the memories of the millions of fanatics across the planet, European or otherwise.

Besides perennial Spanish powerhouse Real Madrid (fifteen-time Final winners as of 2025), who plays domestically in La Liga, the Champions League trophy has been hoisted most frequently by rival squads from top-tier confederations like England's Premier League and Italy's Serie A. Regardless of who's playing in the Final, the atmosphere is unrelentingly passionate, a cacophony of chants and songs building in volume right up to the referee's last whistle. Which happens to be the name of a tall, spritzy libation containing a cavalcade of Europe's tastiest and important spirits from some of its most soccer-mad locales, like English gin, Italian Aperol, French elderflower liqueur, and Spanish cava. Sweet, sour, fizzy, and floral, the Last Whistle simultaneously combines diverse flavors and cultures, perfectly capturing the excitement of the "beautiful game." A seasonally appropriate tipple for the Champions League Final, which usually takes place in late May, it's perfectly delicious in any European climate.

LAST WHISTLE

MAKES 1 DRINK

1 ounce London dry gin, such as Beefeater
¾ ounce fresh lemon juice
½ ounce Aperol
½ ounce elderflower liqueur
½ ounce honey syrup (see page 13)
2 dashes orange bitters
Cava, to top
Club soda, to top
1 lemon twist, for garnish

Combine the gin, lemon juice, Aperol, elderflower liqueur, honey syrup, and orange bitters in a shaker. Add 1 or 2 ice pebbles, shake for 5 seconds, and pour into a large wine glass that has been filled with cracked ice. Top with cava, then club soda. Rub the lemon twist around the rim of the glass, peel side down, then place it in the glass.

AFRICA CUP OF NATIONS

Everything about Africa is big. Covering 11.7 million square miles—almost three times the size of Europe—it contains nearly 20 percent of the world's landmass, divided among fifty-four independent nations. And in most of those, soccer is king, making the biennial Africa Cup of Nations (AFCON) a mandatory viewing experience for millions of football fanatics. The continent's premier international soccer tournament, AFCON debuted in 1957 as a competition between squads from Egypt, Ethiopia, and Sudan, growing rapidly over the years into a twenty-four-team, winner-take-all extravaganza that's considered one of the biggest international events in the sport. In addition to reliably legendary matches on the pitch, the tournament is a unique display of cultural diversity, intense passion, and a rare chance for veteran kickers, many of whom spend their professional careers overseas, to return as hometown heroes, representing the places that birthed their passion for the game.

Soccer in Africa is one of the few universal elements in a region that's home to thousands of divergent languages, spiritual practices, tribal groups, and cuisines influenced by both indigenous traditions and a still-palpable colonial past. Likewise, Africa's drinking habits vary greatly depending on the country, and in many cases, from village to village. But if there's one beverage you're likely to find on every corner of the continent, it's ginger beer. The fizzy refresher, which is often produced domestically, can be enjoyed straight from the bottle or mixed with citrus and bitters in a popular concoction called a shandy. Or, better yet, in delicious libations like the African Ngolo Cocktail. Hailing from Tanzania, host of the 2027 AFCON, this souped-up shandy adds bourbon and maple syrup to the sweet, sour, and slightly spicy medley, creating a depth of flavor that's perfectly suited to Africa's most multifaceted sporting experience.

After retiring, many soccer players remain close to the game, becoming coaches or TV announcers. But Olivier Tébily, who played on the Ivory Coast national team in the 2000 AFCON tournament, decided to go an entirely different route, buying several French vineyards and becoming the first (and so far only) African-born cognac maker.

AFRICAN NGOLO COCKTAIL

MAKES 1 DRINK

2 ounces bourbon
½ ounce fresh lemon juice
½ ounce Amber maple syrup
2 dashes Angostura bitters
Ginger beer, to top
1 piece candied ginger, for garnish

Combine the bourbon, lemon juice, maple syrup, and bitters in a shaker. Add 1 or 2 ice pebbles, shake for 5 seconds, and pour into an ice-filled Collins glass. Top with ginger beer. Skewer the piece of candied ginger with toothpicks and perch it on the rim of the glass.

RUNNING

BOSTON MARATHON

Athens, Greece, can lay claim to the first modern marathon, which was run at the 1896 Summer Olympics. But when it comes to history and tradition, there's nothing like the Boston Marathon. Considered the holy grail of such races, it's currently the oldest, an homage to Paul Revere's Revolutionary journey that's been held every third Monday in April (Patriots' Day) since 1897. Famous for its super strong field—runners must have already run a marathon at a relatively quick pace just to qualify—the daunting, hilly course has witnessed innumerable powerful moments from trailblazers like Kathrine Switzer, Dick Beardsley, and Alberto Salazar, buoyed by some of the wildest and most supportive crowds in all of sports. And the feeling of pride and unity among the runners, spectators, and the city itself—especially since the tragic 2013 Boston Marathon bombings—is more palpable and inspiring than ever before.

Another thing that unites runners is the need for tasty refreshment after a punishing few hours on the racecourse. Sure, you could opt for a boring water or sports drink, but many of today's marathoners—at least the nonprofessionals—prefer to slake their thirst with an ice-cold local beer. In Boston, that usually means Samuel Adams, the flagship brand from Boston Beer Company, the United States' most successful independent brewer. For a cocktail twist on this New England staple, it doesn't get better than a Dog Days of Summer Ale from bartender Tristan Willey. This bright, fruity, and beautifully hued cooler combines always-popular Sam Adams Summer Ale with bourbon, citrus, and sweetly herbaceous spirits like Cherry Heering for a sip that's as memorable as the Boston Marathon. And while April in Boston is rarely described as "summery," the drink's seasonal ale base goes on sale in early March, giving you plenty of time to stock up before race day.

If you're getting secondhand Marathon-Day exhaustion and don't feel like whipping up a cocktail, you can always grab a Samuel Adams 26.2 Brew, which has been dubbed the Boston Marathon's official beverage since debuting in 2012. It's a gose-style ale that, according to the brewery, "features light cereal notes from malted and unmalted wheat, a soft mouthfeel, and a touch of peppery spice—ideal for post-race celebrations."

DOG DAYS OF SUMMER ALE

MAKES 1 DRINK

½ ounce bourbon
½ ounce sweet vermouth
½ ounce Cherry Heering
½ ounce fresh lemon juice
8 ounces Samuel Adams Summer Ale
1 lemon wedge, for garnish

Combine the bourbon, vermouth, Cherry Heering, and lemon juice in a shaker. Add 1 or 2 small ice pebbles, shake for 5 seconds, and pour into a tall glass over ice. Top with the Samuel Adams Summer Ale. Perch the lemon wedge on the rim of the glass.

WORLD MARATHON CHALLENGE

For an average recreational runner, completing a marathon may be the pinnacle of athletic achievement. For the exceptionally fit lunatics attempting to complete the annual World Marathon Challenge, that's just a Tuesday. Perhaps the greatest physical and logistical feat in road racing, the WMC requires participants to complete seven marathons on seven continents—in only seven days. And yes, that includes Antarctica, which happens to be the race's first leg. Runners take ten bone-chilling loops around the 4.2-kilometer perimeter of Novo Air Base before being whisked on chartered planes to courses in Africa, Australia, Asia, Europe, South America, and, finally, North America, running a total of 183 miles and spending about sixty-eight hours in the air.

Novelist J. G. Ballard wrote that "madness is the key to freedom." That must be particularly true in the endurance sports community, as the number of long-distance runners looking to test the limits of their abilities in the World Marathon Challenge has grown steadily since the event was first held in 2015. Like Michael Wardian, who averaged an absurd 2:45:57 per marathon during his record-setting 2017 performance. Or David Kilgore, who, after winning all seven marathons in the 2023 edition of the WMC, immediately hopped on a plane to compete in a 52-kilometer trail race in New Zealand.

There's nothing wrong with being so obsessed with running seven marathons, per se, but it doesn't give you much time to prepare cocktails. Thankfully, the most iconic "7"-themed drink is also the easiest to make. A combination of Seagram's 7 Whiskey and 7UP, the 7&7 is a classic highball that's delighted time-strapped drinkers for decades, peaking in popularity, appropriately enough, in the 1970s. This bright and citrusy refresher is still worth a run to the liquor store—though maybe not 26.2 miles in Antarctic temperatures.

Often described as the "quintessential dive bar drink," the 7&7 was largely responsible for Seagram's 7 becoming the first liquor brand to sell more than 100 million cases, according to booze historian and former Seagram's employee Arthur Shapiro.

7&7

MAKES 1 DRINK

2 ounces Seagram's 7 Crown Blended Whiskey
7UP, to top

Add the Seagram's 7 Crown Blended Whiskey to an ice-filled Collins glass. Top with 7UP and stir gently with a long-handled spoon for 5 or 6 seconds.

THE SPEED PROJECT

Unruly. Unsanctioned. Off-grid. Invite-only. Spectator-free. Those probably aren't the first adjectives you'd use to describe any of the world's major road races. Except for one: the Speed Project, a brutal 340-mile relay where teams of six runners hoof it from the Santa Monica Pier in Southern California to the "Welcome to Fabulous Las Vegas" sign, traversing diverse and always relentless terrain such as the Hollywood Hills, an airplane graveyard in the Mojave Desert, and Death Valley National Park, all without a fixed course, rest stops, hotel breaks, or any monetary incentive. Yet this seemingly insane DIY event, founded in 2013 by mavericks Nils Arend and Blue Benadum, continues to attract top athletes every year due to the mysterious and wild aura that surrounds it.

Between running for miles in the sweltering desert heat and riding in team RVs where, according to runner Riley Wolff, everything is "covered in a layer of sweat," the Speed Project's participants partake in a journey that's often as smelly as it is challenging. Which is why the traditional beer and champagne shower under the "Welcome to Las Vegas" sign for the winning team is particularly refreshing for athletes who haven't washed properly in days.

Like traditional road racing, the cocktail world is also full of long-standing customs: how to use certain ingredients and in which proportions, what flavors should and shouldn't be combined, et cetera. But every so often, a drink will emerge that audaciously challenges these conventions—a liquid Speed Project, if you will—and in doing so, change the way we look at drink-making. One fine recent example is the Bitter Giuseppe from Chicago bartender Stephen Cole. Unlike most Manhattan variations that feature whiskey as a base spirit, this bittersweet beauty relies on Cynar, a distinctively complex Italian amaro notably made with artichokes. Usually sipped over ice or used in a supporting role, Cole allows Cynar to fully shine here, aided by bright notes of orange bitters and a hint of fresh lemon juice (another rarity in stirred drinks), for a truly unique aperitivo cocktail that you won't have to run hundreds of miles through scorching desert to experience.

BITTER GIUSEPPE

MAKES 1 DRINK

2 ounces Cynar
1 ounce sweet vermouth
¼ ounce fresh lemon juice
6 dashes orange bitters
1 lemon twist, for garnish

Combine the Cynar, vermouth, lemon juice, and orange bitters in a double rocks glass. Add ice and stir with a long-handled spoon for 5 or 6 seconds. Rub the lemon twist around the rim of the glass, peel side down, then place it in the glass.

22
91

BAY TO BREAKERS

The daily hurdles competitive runners face—staying motivated during training sessions, maintaining a strict nutritional regimen, overcoming fears of failure and injury—can make it easy to forget why most of them started running in the first place: It was fun. That feeling of unbridled joy is easy to recapture at San Francisco's Bay to Breakers, a road race unlike any other, where living it up is always of the utmost importance.

Founded to raise the city's spirits after the devastating 1906 earthquake, the 12-kilometer test starts near San Francisco Bay and finishes at the Pacific Ocean, where breaking waves crash onto Ocean Beach. It's one of the world's largest sporting events, with more than 100,000 party-loving participants, many of whom come decked out in hilariously elaborate costumes (or, occasionally, in nothing but a pair of sneakers). Live bands and droves of boisterous, well-lubricated spectators add to the day's infectious energy, which, despite efforts by local government killjoys to tone down some of the race's more risqué aspects, remains intrinsic to San Francisco's cultural heart.

The City by the Bay isn't just the backdrop to one of running's most idiosyncratic festivities. It's also been a bastion of West Coast cocktail elegance for more than 150 years. One nineteenth-century local classic is the Pisco Punch, a potent blend of pisco, pineapple, lime, and gum arabica attributed to Duncan Nicol, proprietor of the Bank Exchange & Billiard Saloon. Over the years, the drink, described as having "the kick of a roped steer," achieved legendary status and was praised by the likes of Jack London and Rudyard Kipling. And though its original specifications have been lost, the recipe below is a faithful re-creation of its iconic flavor profile, a taste that's as uniquely San Franciscan as running a 12k in your birthday suit.

Besides being a staple of the San Francisco bar scene, the Pisco Punch, in all likelihood, directly influenced the course of American literary history, as Mark Twain, a regular at the Bank Exchange & Billiard Saloon, allegedly met and befriended the man who would go on to inspire the character of Tom Sawyer while knocking back many rounds of the drink.

PISCO PUNCH

MAKES 1 DRINK

2 ounces pisco
1 ounce fresh pineapple juice
½ ounce fresh lime juice
½ ounce gum arabica syrup, such as Liber & Co. Classic Gum Syrup
1 pineapple slice, for garnish

Combine the pisco, pineapple juice, lime juice, and gum arabica syrup in an ice-filled shaker. Shake vigorously for 15 seconds and strain over ice into a double rocks glass. Perch the pineapple slice on the rim of the glass.

GOLF

THE MASTERS

Several telltale sights and sounds herald the arrival of spring each year. Longer days and lighter evenings. Blooming flowers. Buzzing bees and chirping birds. And the roar of the crowd along the pristine fairways of Georgia's Augusta National Golf Club. Held each April since 1934, the Masters Tournament is considered by many to be golf's most prestigious event and the sport's only major championship played on the same course each year. Renowned for its gorgeous yet treacherous layout, as well as many holes featuring deceptively serene floral names such as "Flowering Peach" and "Yellow Jasmine," Augusta National is home to dozens of unique rituals, most famously the post-tournament ceremony in which the winning golfer is presented with one of the club's distinctive green jackets by the previous year's champion.

Some of the most beloved Masters traditions extend beyond the golf course, originating in the many concession stands that line the property: specifically, feasting on pimento cheese and egg salad sandwiches, simple yet undeniably delicious snacks that have satiated innumerable fans, caddies, and players for decades. And of course, enjoying the tournament's signature beverage, the Azalea Cocktail. Named for the rosy-colored Georgia state flower whose impressive blooms dot the course (the thirteenth hole is also named "Azalea"), this similarly pink-hued refresher has been a staple at the tournament for several decades. And while it's unclear when or where it was first served—some sources point to Augusta's main clubhouse or one of its members-only VIP bars—the Azalea is the perfect sweet, sour, and fruity companion for watching golf's most revered pageant, regardless of who you're rooting for.

You might be tempted to spruce up a Masters-inspired cocktail with an azalea flower garnish, but please don't. Though they make for excellent scenery, the plant's petals are highly toxic to both humans and pets.

AZALEA COCKTAIL

MAKES 1 DRINK

2 ounces gin or vodka
2 ounces fresh pineapple juice
¾ ounce fresh lemon juice
¼ ounce grenadine (or pomegranate syrup (see page 13)
1 lemon wheel, for garnish

Combine the spirit of choice, pineapple juice, lemon juice, and grenadine in an ice-filled shaker. Shake vigorously for 15 seconds and strain into a tall glass filled with ice. Place the lemon wheel in the glass beside the ice.

U.S. OPEN

For golf-loving American families, no Father's Day is complete without a few hours spent watching the final riveting round of the U.S. Open. America's oldest major tournament is always played the third week in June, but that's only a small part of why it's special. Considered by many to be the toughest test in the sport, the championship is played on long, narrow courses smattered with viciously tilting greens and diabolically unkempt rough, where shooting even par is considered a massive achievement, and where all-time greats like Walter Hagen, Jack Nicklaus, Tiger Woods, and Rory McIlroy have frequently made names for themselves or solidified their legendary statures.

No single player was more famous in the tournament's early years than the legendary Bobby Jones. American golf's greatest amateur competitor (and a full-time practicing lawyer during his career), Jones won four U.S. Open titles from 1923 to 1930, finished in second place four times, and was the author of myriad thrilling moments, including an overtime-clinching 12-foot putt at the 1929 Open at New York's Winged Foot Golf Course that, at the time, was called the most clutch shot in history. He's also the namesake of a delightful libation that's a close cousin of venerated golf-related beverages like the Arnold Palmer (an equal-parts combo of iced tea and lemonade) and its vodka-spiked variation, the John Daly. The Bobby Jones Cocktail employs those same refreshing flavors and adds peach-infused bourbon and peach bitters—a nod to Jones's Georgia roots—alongside hints of aromatized wine and brown sugar, for a smooth and summery treat that's as satisfying as a tap-in birdie on the eighteenth green.

In 2022, the United States Golf Association partnered with Dewar's Blended Scotch Whisky to create an official cocktail for the U.S. Open. The Dewar's Wedge—a simple blend of scotch, lemonade, and club soda—never really took off after that year's tournament. But it's not a bad summertime refresher if you've got those ingredients lying around.

Recipe follows

BOBBY JONES COCKTAIL

MAKES 1 DRINK

2 ounces Peach-Infused Bourbon (recipe follows)
½ ounce fresh lemon juice
¼ ounce Cocchi Americano
¼ ounce Demerara syrup (see simple syrup, page 13)
2 dashes peach bitters
Unsweetened iced tea, to top
1 peach wedge, for garnish
1 lemon wedge, for garnish

Combine the bourbon, lemon juice, Cocchi Americano, Demerara syrup, and peach bitters in a shaker. Add 1 or 2 ice pebbles, shake for 5 seconds, and pour into an ice-filled Collins glass. Top with iced tea. Skewer the peach wedge and lemon wedge with a toothpick and perch them on the rim of the glass.

Peach-Infused Bourbon

MAKES APPROXIMATELY 26 OUNCES

2 ripe peaches
1 750-ml bottle bourbon

Wash and slice the peaches and place the slices in a large mason jar. Fill the jar with bourbon. Cover tightly and store in a cool, dry place for 4 to 5 days. Pour the contents of the mason jar through a fine-mesh strainer into an airtight container. Discard the peach slices. Store in a cool, dry place for up to 6 months or in the refrigerator for up to 1 year.

PGA CHAMPIONSHIP

To the casual observer, the PGA Championship might not garner the same excitement as, or possess the near-mythological aura of, say, the Masters or the Open Championship. But for golf fanatics, the sport's second-youngest major tournament is must-see TV. Established in 1916 by the then newly formed Professional Golfers' Association of America, the championship was the first officially sanctioned competition reserved exclusively for professionals, who felt overshadowed by that era's more popular amateur stars. Today, the PGA boasts the strongest field in golf, featuring more players in the top one hundred of the Official World Golf Ranking than any other major, and also has a long history of epic final-round duels, which may be partially due to the tournament's unique three-hole aggregate playoff (in the event of a tie after seventy-two holes of regulation play), a format considered by many pros to be the most equitable and exciting in the sport.

Players of every skill level share a similar passion for drowning sorrows or toasting triumphs at the nineteenth hole. A slang term for any pub or restaurant near a golf course—or often in the clubhouse itself—where golfers commiserate after a standard eighteen-hole round, it's also the inspiration for a delightful martini variation of the same name. The Nineteenth Hole cocktail, which was first served in New York around the same time the PGA was forming, starts with a gin and dry vermouth formula like its classic predecessor, then livens things up with a touch of Angostura bitters and sweet vermouth for a slightly brighter, more complex cocktail experience. You don't have to be an expert mixologist to stir up one of these simple yet classy tipples, but you'll certainly feel like a pro after sipping a few.

To experience the most famous nineteenth hole in golf, you'll need to travel to the Old Course in St Andrews, Scotland, where the Jigger Inn has overlooked the seventeenth green since 1852. The pub's seemingly cocktail-related name actually refers to an obsolete golf club that was a very low lofted iron with a shortened shaft, rather than the tool used for measuring out alcohol. That said, the inn's mixed drinks and exclusive Jigger Ale are both top-notch.

Recipe follows

NINETEENTH HOLE

MAKES 1 DRINK

1¾ ounces gin
1 ounce dry vermouth
1 barspoon sweet vermouth
2 dashes Angostura bitters
1 olive, for garnish

Combine the gin, both vermouths, and the bitters in an ice-filled mixing glass. Stir with a long-handled spoon for 25 to 30 seconds and strain into a martini glass or coupe. Drop the olive into the glass.

THE OPEN CHAMPIONSHIP

The oldest golf tournament in the world, the Open Championship (also known as the British Open) is considered—arguably—the sport's preeminent event, famous for the punishing, windswept "links" style courses on which it's played, the Claret Jug trophy, and countless iconic moments during its more than 160-year history. Originally played at Scotland's Prestwick Golf Club in 1860, the championship rotates each July between a select few coastal venues like England's Royal St George's and Northern Ireland's Royal Portrush.

But the most celebrated of these, by far, is the very place where golf was born in the early 1400s: the Old Course at St Andrew's, a name whispered with religious reverence by the innumerable golfers who have hacked their way through its treacherous fairways. Like three-time Open champion Sir Henry Cotton, who said, "Winning the Open Championship can turn a good player into a star, but winning the Open at St Andrews can turn a great player into a legend."

One popular (but unlikely) legend about golf's origins claims that the reason for there being eighteen holes on a golf course is that there are eighteen shots in a fifth of scotch whisky, which, according to many early proponents of the game, was the perfect amount of booze for a day on the links.

Perfecting a winning drink recipe can also grant you legendary bartender status, at least in the eyes of the guests at your next cocktail party. Look no further than the Smash, a simple mixture of spirit, muddled lemon, muddled mint, and sugar that's likely older than the Open and first appeared in print in the 1887 edition of Jerry Thomas's *The Bartender's Guide*. Originally made with bourbon, the flavor combination also works amazingly well with scotch (and just about anything else in your liquor cabinet). You'll need a good muddler—the bartending equivalent of a trusty nine iron—and a bit of elbow grease to release the rich, cooling oils in the lemon and mint, but this tasty and citrusy standby is well worth the effort.

WHISKY SMASH

MAKES 1 DRINK

2 ounces blended scotch
¾ ounce simple syrup (see page 13)
5 lemon wedges
1 small handful mint leaves
1 sprig mint, for garnish

Combine the scotch, simple syrup, lemon wedges, and mint leaves in a shaker. Muddle thoroughly, add ice, and shake vigorously for 15 seconds. Strain into a double rocks glass filled with cracked ice. Place the mint sprig in the glass beside the ice.

TENNIS

WIMBLEDON

In a sports world obsessed with change, where alterations to major rules, playoff formats, and team names are the norm, adhering to tradition can, ironically, feel a bit refreshing. It doesn't get more old-school than Wimbledon, the world's oldest tennis tournament and the only major contest still fought on grass, the sport's original playing surface. The most prestigious event at London's All England Lawn Tennis and Croquet Club—and, according to most authorities, at any tennis club—retains much of the character and appearance from its first incarnation, such as its royal patronage, the all-white dress code for both male and female players, the selection of ball boys and girls from local high schools, and shockingly minimal advertising from major brand sponsors. And, given that the tournament's history of unforgettable performances by all-time greats like John McEnroe, Martina Navratilova, Andy Murray, and Serena Williams has shown no signs of letting up, it begs the question: Why mess with a good thing?

Wimbledon's official snack, strawberries and cream, and its signature beverage, the Pimm's Cup, prove that tradition can feel good and taste even better. The latter, a quintessential English tipple that mixes Pimm's No. 1—a gin-infused herbal liqueur created by oyster monger James Pimm in the early 1800s—with copious muddled berries and either citrusy soda or ginger ale, has been sipped at the All England Club since the first tournament in 1877. Today, it's still an effective summertime quencher, enjoyed by 300,000 attendees each year, whether sitting in the (relatively) cheap seats, sidled up at the club's seminal Pimm's Bar, or perched alongside the iconic Centre Court in the British monarch's private box. You don't need to be a king, queen, or grass-court superstar to enjoy one of these fruity festivities in a glass, but it'll certainly make you feel like royalty.

Pimm's No. 1 Cup isn't just a perfect summertime drink because of its taste. Like tonic water, it contains a chemical called quinine, which is commonly used to treat malaria. Take that, mosquitoes!

PIMM'S CUP

MAKES 1 DRINK

2 ounces Pimm's No. 1
3 thin cucumber slices
1 lemon wedge
1 lime wedge
1 thin orange slice
1 strawberry, halved
1 blackberry
1 brandied cherry
Lemon-lime soda, to top
1 sprig mint, for garnish

Combine the Pimm's, 1 cucumber slice, the lemon wedge, lime wedge, orange slice, strawberry, blackberry, and brandied cherry in a shaker. Muddle, then pour into a Collins glass. Add ice and top with the lemon-lime soda. Skewer the remaining 2 cucumber slices with the mint sprig and perch them on the rim of the glass.

U.S. OPEN

It's well known among tennis lovers that the U.S. Open is different. Some point to the prize money—the biggest purse in the sport—or that it's the last major event of the year, which raises the stakes and puts extra pressure on players who haven't won yet. But at the end of the day, as any New York City Realtor will tell you, it's all about location, location, location. There are few, if any, sporting events that can match the electric courtside atmosphere of Queens' USTA Billie Jean King National Tennis Center during the two weeks before and after Labor Day, when it's filled with both boisterous New Yorkers and die-hard fans from every corner of the globe. Especially during the late-night matches at Arthur Ashe Stadium, the center's main venue. With a capacity of more than 23,000, it's the largest tennis stadium in the world and—as those who have gone toe to toe in thrilling battles on the hard court will tell you—it sure sounds like it.

The tournament's ambience can be at least partially attributed to the fact that the City That Never Sleeps is also the City That Never Turns Down a Good Beverage. Since 2006, fans have had no problem staying lubricated thanks to the U.S. Open's official drink, the Honey Deuce. Created by restaurateur Nick Mautone in collaboration with Grey Goose (and named after 40-40 tie score that's called a "deuce" in tennis terminology), the combination of fresh lemonade spiked with vodka and raspberry liqueur, served with crushed ice and garnished with scoops of honeydew melon that look like adorable little tennis balls, is pure late-summer perfection. Even if you can't join the throngs in NYC, you'll be able to whip up one of these at home faster than a game-winning serve.

From 2015 to 2019, vendors at the U.S. Open estimated that they served more than 1 million Honey Deuces. That's over 3 million melon balls and about 37,000 bottles of Grey Goose.

HONEY DEUCE

MAKES 1 DRINK

1½ ounces vodka, such as Grey Goose
3 ounces lemonade, preferably fresh
½ ounce raspberry liqueur, such as Chambord
3 honeydew melon balls, fresh or frozen, for garnish

Fill a double rocks glass two-thirds of the way with cubed or crushed ice. Add the vodka, then top with the lemonade and raspberry liqueur. Do not stir. Add a straw and top with more ice. Skewer the honeydew melon balls and drape them over the rim of the glass.

FRENCH OPEN

Unless you're really into pottery, you probably don't spend a lot of time thinking about clay. But where tennis court surfaces are concerned, it can be a huge cause for apprehension. Especially at the French Open. Also called Roland-Garros (in honor of the World War I aviator) and held in the Parisian stadium of the same name, it's the only major event played on clay and, due to that porous substance's unique characteristics and the event's lengthy format, is considered the most physically demanding tennis championship. Since its founding in 1891, the tournament has been the Achilles' heel for otherwise dominant, hard-serving legends like Pete Sampras, as the soft ground tends to slow the pace of the ball, nullifying any strength-based advantages. Conversely, the Open has been a boon to finesse players, none more so than Rafael Nadal, whose fourteen wins from 2005 to 2014 constitute an unprecedented feat in tournament play.

Whichever style of tennis you prefer, the matches at Stade Roland Garros are guaranteed to provide hours of action that's unlike anything else in the game. If you can't score tickets to Paris's hottest late-spring spectacle—and its swanky concession stands brimming with deliciously on-brand French snacks and beverages—you can still treat yourself to the Open's signature drink, the Ace Royal. While its origins are unknown, the champagne-forward, citrusy cooler is, without a doubt, one of the most titillating bubble-based libations around. Infusions of fresh basil and cucumber add pleasant earthy and vegetal notes to this icy, fragrant, can't-miss quencher, which works wonders after sweating it out for a few sets on the court, regardless of the surface type.

In a move that shocked the libation-loving French tennis community, Roland-Garros permanently outlawed drinking in the stands before the 2024 event, the first major tennis tournament to do so, following a trend at many European soccer stadiums. Fans need not be so distraught, as they can still step outside the venue and grab a leisurely drink from the concessions or one of the roving vendors selling beer from kegs strapped to their backs.

ACE ROYAL

MAKES 1 DRINK

1 ounce fresh lime juice
¾ ounce simple syrup (see page 13)
6 fresh basil leaves
5 thin cucumber slices
Champagne, to top

Combine the lime juice, simple syrup, 5 basil leaves, and 3 cucumber slices in an ice-filled shaker. Shake for 5 seconds and dump the entire contents of the shaker into a double rocks glass. Fill the glass with more cracked ice (if necessary) and top with champagne. Tuck the remaining 2 cucumber slices and basil leaf in the glass alongside the ice.

AUSTRALIAN OPEN

Achieving a calendar-year Grand Slam is considered the holy grail of tennis. And understandably, attempting to sweep the sport's four major singles titles in one season can put an impossible strain on the mental and physical health of those attempting such a feat. Those weary vibes, however, are blissfully absent at the Australian Open, the first leg of the journey that takes place in January, when most players arrive from a restful offseason feeling healthy and motivated and ready to soak up the Southern Hemisphere sun in the scenic city of Melbourne. The weather is far from the only draw, however. The AO, as it's called, has always been known for innovation, most visibly in the "champions walk," in which players enter the court via a corridor lined with illuminated pillars displaying the names of former champions. And the crowds are electric, particularly when a local player reaches the final rounds, such as in 2022, when Ashleigh Barty became the first Aussie to win a singles title at the tournament in forty-four years.

Born minutes from Melbourne Park, the AO's storied venue, Pat Cash is another Australian who's left an indelible mark on the sport. Famous for climbing into the stands after winning the 1987 Wimbledon title, he's become, since retiring, a major teacher and promoter of tennis worldwide. He's also credited with inventing the Pat Cash Grand Slam Cocktail at the Buccament Bay Resort on St. Vincent, a Caribbean island whose overproof-rum-loving lifestyle aligns with the tournament Roger Federer once dubbed the "Happy Slam." Attempting to slam—or even slowly sip—this divine yet dastardly, coconutty blend of three rums and tropical juices won't help your tennis game, but it will make the Australian Open a lot of fun to watch. As if you needed any more encouragement.

In 2019, the organizers of the Australian Open inked one of the biggest sponsorship deals in tennis history, partnering with Luzhou Laojiao, one of China's largest producers of that country's national spirit, baijiu. Most of the subsequent advertising focused on Guojiao (or National Cellar) 1573, the company's premier product, a traditional baijiu made by fermenting sorghum in an earthen pit (the oldest pits at Luzhou Laojiao date to 1573) using a mixed culture of yeasts, bacteria, and fungi, then distilling the fermented grain and maturing the resulting clear spirit in large ceramic jars for years before bottling at 110 proof.

PAT CASH GRAND SLAM COCKTAIL

MAKES 1 DRINK

1 ounce coconut rum
¾ ounce overproof white rum
¾ ounce aged rum
1 ounce fresh orange juice
1 ounce fresh pineapple juice
¼ ounce fresh lime juice
¼ ounce pomegranate syrup (see page 13)
¼ ounce cane syrup
1 sprig mint, for garnish
1 lime wedge, for garnish

Combine the rums, juices, and syrups in a shaker. Add 1 or 2 ice pebbles, shake for 5 seconds, and pour into a tall glass or tiki mug filled two-thirds of the way with crushed ice. Add a straw and top with more ice. Place the mint sprig and lime wedge on top of the ice.

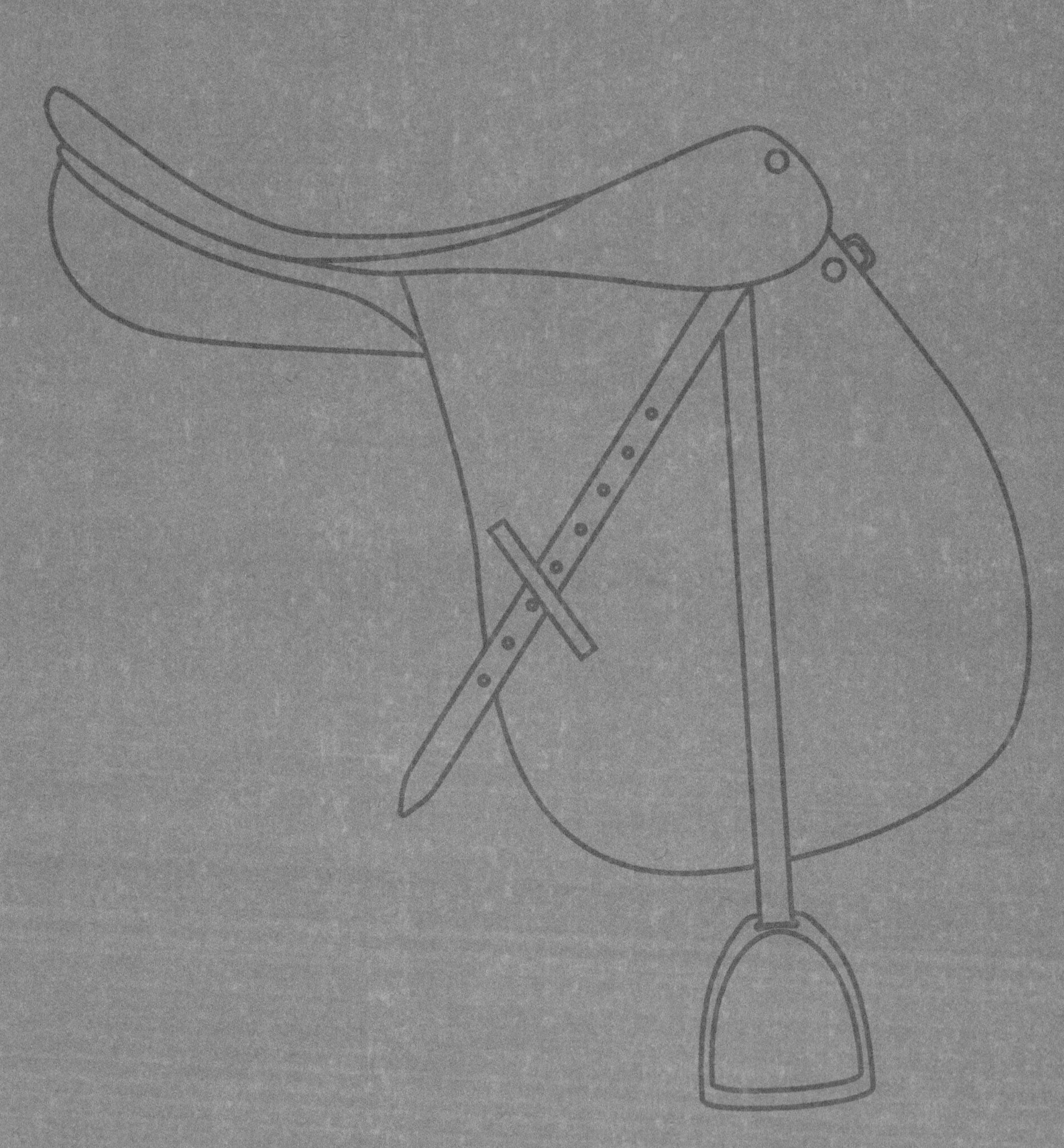

HORSE RACING

KENTUCKY DERBY

The most exciting two minutes in sports. The Super Bowl of horse racing. America's greatest race. There's no shortage of superlatives for the Kentucky Derby, the United States' oldest—and to many, most beloved—continuously run annual sporting event, held on the first Saturday of May at Louisville's Churchill Downs racetrack since 1875. And for good reason. The first leg of the Triple Crown of Thoroughbred Racing has been the stage for a slew of sensational moments, such as Secretariat's epic 1973 performance in which the big red colt rallied late to finish the 1¼-mile course in record time, or Mine That Bird shockingly winning the 2009 race as a 50–1 longshot. Yet the action on the track is only part of the appeal. The crowds of 150,000 or more are treated to a display of pomp and Southern hospitality unlike any other, from the lilting notes of "Old Kentucky Home" and the over-the-top fashion to the ubiquitous mint juleps that are never out of reach.

The earliest notable American cocktail, the Mint Julep was also the first popular drink served with ice, as its origins coincided with the rise of commercial icehouses that could ship their blocks around the world. When the manufactured ice ran out, frantic bartenders were known to collect hailstones or run with icepicks to the nearest frozen pond to appease their thirsty customers.

The derby's official beverage since 1939, considered by many whiskey aficionados to be the apex of herbal-infused refreshment, has been a staple at the bars, boudoirs, and back porches of the Southeastern U.S. since at least the 1770s. Originally made with brandy and sipped for medicinal purposes, a familiar version of the julep—an invigorating nectar of bourbon, fresh mint, sugar, and lots of crushed ice—became associated with the Kentucky horse-racing scene in the 1820s, when julep cups, traditionally made of sterling silver, were awarded as trophies to winning jockeys, a perfect marriage of Kentucky's two best-known industries, and a practice that continues today. Though you could easily down one quicker than a thoroughbred's lap around the track, to truly appreciate this sneakily boozy masterpiece, it's best to take it slow.

MINT JULEP

MAKES 1 DRINK

Handful of mint leaves, plus 1 sprig for garnish
2½ ounces bourbon
¼ ounce simple syrup (see page 13)
1 sugar cube

Gently squeeze the mint leaves in your hand (to release their fragrance) and drop them into a traditional silver julep cup. Add the bourbon, simple syrup, and sugar cube to the cup. Muddle lightly to break up the sugar cube (but not to bruise the mint) and fill the cup two-thirds of the way with crushed ice. Stir with a swizzle stick, then add a straw and top with more crushed ice. Garnish with the mint sprig.

PREAKNESS STAKES

The Kentucky Derby has name recognition for casual fans and the Belmont Stakes determines any potential Triple Crown winner. But for many horse-racing diehards, especially those living in Maryland, the Preakness Stakes is the year's main event. Held since 1873 at Baltimore's Pimlico Race Course in late May, the 9.5-furlong sprint is so ingrained in the equine-crazy culture that the city's original NFL franchise was named the Colts in its honor. That love has begotten some truly over-the-top traditions beyond the action on the track. Like the post-race "painting of the vane," in which an artist climbs the replica cupola of Pimlico's Old Clubhouse that sits in the current course's infield, to paint the iconic horse-and-jockey weathervane that sits atop it to match the silks of that year's winner. Following that is the presentation of the Tiffany & Co.–designed Woodlawn Vase, which, with an estimated value of around $1 million, is called "The Most Valuable Trophy in Sports." Take that, Kentucky!

The Preakness is perhaps most associated, visually, with the state flower of Maryland, the black-eyed Susan, a daisy-like plant with yellow petals and a dark central cone, whose distinctive hues dominate the floral blanket that's draped on the winning horse. It's also the name of the signature cocktail that's served at the race, though the recipe seems to have changed more frequently than the jockeys at the starting gate. Older, pineapple-heavy versions mostly favored the dreaded sour mix, with base spirits ranging from bourbon to peach schnapps to vodka. The following iteration, adapted from David Solmonson's *The 12 Bottle Bar* (2014), preserves the appropriate golden-hued color scheme, but favors fresh juices and a surprisingly copacetic combo of two rums and rye whiskey, with a delightfully rich, molasses-influenced nose.

If you're looking for something to nosh on while downing Black-Eyed Susans, you can't go wrong with crab cakes. Those succulent, golden lumps of blue crab meat, breadcrumbs, mayonnaise, mustard, eggs, and Old Bay seasoning are the unofficial state food of Maryland, with several thousand of the deep-fried delicacies sold at the Preakness each year.

BLACK-EYED SUSAN

MAKES 1 DRINK

2 ounces fresh pineapple juice
1 ounce rye whiskey
1 ounce white rum
½ ounce fresh lemon juice
½ ounce simple syrup (see page 13)
1 barspoon Cointreau
½ ounce black rum
1 orange wheel, for garnish
1 cocktail cherry, for garnish

Combine the pineapple juice, rye, rum, lemon juice, simple syrup, and Cointreau in a shaker. Pour into a tall glass filled two-thirds of the way with crushed ice. Float the black rum, add a straw, and top with more crushed ice. Perch the orange wheel and cocktail cherry on top of the ice.

BELMONT STAKES

The Belmont Stakes, the "Third Jewel of the Triple Crown," is also the longest of horse-racing's hallowed trifecta, a full 1.5-mile lap around the impressively massive Belmont Park in Elmont, New York. Winning here is no easy feat for any horse, let alone three-year-old thoroughbreds that have already won the Kentucky Derby and the Preakness, saddled by jockeys who feel the indescribable pressure of completing a Triple Crown sweep, something that's only been accomplished once every twelve years, on average, since all three races were first run simultaneously in 1875. Yet even in most years, when that rare achievement is out of reach, the "Test of Champions" is still a joy to behold, a punishing test on what's considered by many experts to be the United States' fairest track, where tactical speed is at a premium and where it's almost impossible to overcome a poor start.

Race-wise, not much has changed since the Belmont debuted in 1867. The same can't be said for the signature beverages to which spectators have been treated over the years. "Treat" may be a poor descriptor for the oldest of these, the White Carnation, named for the blanket of eponymous flowers bestowed upon the winning horse. A sordid vodka and peach schnapps affair that was described as "nigh undrinkable" in a 1997 *New York Times* article, it was replaced that year by the only slightly less-questionable Belmont Breeze, a hodgepodge of bourbon, sherry, and abundant juices that the same paper described as a "refined trashcan." Thankfully, the culinary cadre at the "Third Jewel" seems to have finally gotten things right in as many tries in 2011 with the Belmont Jewel, a refreshingly simple and straightforward bourbon sour variation with the slightest of fruity finishes. A major win for the palates and stomachs of horse-racing fans everywhere.

Most athletes keep their bodies in pristine condition before a competition, though many have been known to enjoy a postgame libation or two. That's not the case with 1973 Belmont Stakes and Triple Crown winner Secretariat. Whether on the track or in the pasture, the all-time greatest racehorse only drank Mountain Valley Spring Water, personally delivered to him via company truck.

BELMONT JEWEL

MAKES 1 DRINK

2 ounces bourbon
¾ ounce fresh lemon juice
¾ ounce simple syrup (see page 13)
¼ ounce pomegranate syrup (see page 13)
1 lemon twist, for garnish

Combine the bourbon, lemon juice, simple syrup, and pomegranate syrup in an ice-filled shaker. Shake vigorously for 15 seconds and strain over ice into a double rocks glass. Rub the lemon twist around the rim of the glass, peel side down, then place it in the glass beside the ice.

RUGBY

SIX NATIONS CHAMPIONSHIP

It's often been said that proximity makes for the best rivalries. That's certainly the case in the Six Nations Championship, an annual rugby union tournament held by teams representing England, Ireland, Scotland, Wales, Italy, and France. Launched in 1883 as a battle for bragging rights between the four British Home Nations (which then included Ireland), it's one of the oldest and most prestigious competitions in the sport, expanding in recent years to include teams from Western European neighbors, as well as a women's tournament, adding to the international drama.

Starting in February and concluding in March, each team plays every other team once and the nation with the most points is crowned champion; achieving a rare Grand Slam—by defeating all other teams—is the ultimate conquest. Teams compete in individual rivalry matches throughout the tournament, like the coveted Calcutta Cup between England and Scotland, assuring constant intrigue for countries who, although geographically close, have remarkably unique cultures, something that their vociferous fan bases make known whenever presented with an opportunity.

One thing these somewhat divergent locales do share is a venerable love for spirits and, in most cases, a long history of producing them. Irish and Scotch whiskies are worldwide favorites, and many discerning drinkers would engage in a rugby scrum to get their hands on their favorite French liqueurs and Italian amari, prized for centuries for their one-of-a-kind bouquets that come in an endless array of floral and herbaceous overtones. Fine examples of these tipples factor into the Six Nations Slammer, a hefty highball that also features English cider and Welsh honey (though local versions of these work just fine). Robust, semisweet, and a tad spicy, it's a great reminder of the surprising harmony that can result from bringing together seemingly far-flung ingredients (or nations).

Though many of today's players are more likely to sip on smoothies than ales, rugby and drinking culture have long been intertwined, resulting in some interesting (and now defunct) pregame rituals. Like the English team in the 1990s holding secret "Thursday Night Wine Clubs" in their hotel less than forty-eight hours before Six Nations matches, tasking rookies with disposing of the evidence.

SIX NATIONS SLAMMER

MAKES 1 DRINK

¾ ounce blended scotch
¾ ounce Irish whiskey
½ ounce elderflower liqueur
½ ounce fresh lemon juice
½ ounce apple cider
⅜ ounce ginger syrup (see page 13)
⅜ ounce honey syrup (see page 13)
¼ ounce Italian amaro
Club soda, to top
1 piece candied ginger, for garnish

Combine the scotch, Irish whiskey, elderflower liqueur, lemon juice, apple cider, ginger syrup, and honey syrup in a shaker. Add 1 or 2 ice pebbles, shake for 5 seconds, and pour into an ice-filled Collins glass. Float the Italian amaro and top with club soda. Skewer the piece of candied ginger with toothpicks and perch it on the rim of the glass.

THE RUGBY CHAMPIONSHIP

The Southern Hemisphere only contains about 13 percent of the world's population. However, the lower half of the planet (depending on where you're standing) is home to an exponentially greater proportion of the world's top rugby union-playing countries. Four of these global powers—South Africa, New Zealand, Australia, and Argentina—compete annually in the Rugby Championship, a massively viewed, double round-robin tournament where national pride and the honor of storied rugby traditions lie at the heart of every titanic clash. Unlike their European counterparts like longtime Six Nations rivals England and Scotland, the best Southern teams only played sporadically until 1996, when the championship's first iteration, the Tri Nation Series, debuted. Yet despite its relatively brief history, the Rugby Championship provides plenty of intrigue, intensity, hotly contested side quests—like the Freedom Cup between New Zealand and South Africa—and superior gameplay that's unlike anything else on either side of the equator.

Much like its first-rate rugby union squads, several of the Southern Hemisphere's traditional spirits have begun to dominate the global scene, especially grape-based pisco and sugarcane-distilled cachaça. And while both of those lauded liquors hail from South America, they're enjoyed on each of the Rugby Championship's representatives' continents, particularly in Australia and New Zealand cocktail hotbeds like Melbourne and Auckland. They also form an addictively smooth alliance in the Southern Hemisphere, an absolute kicker of a daiquiri variation from Kay Oakley. The camaraderie, an important element in rugby union competition as well as in the best cocktails, is amplified here with the beautiful mingling of pisco's floral, earthy, and fruity aromatics with the crisp, subtle sweetness of cachaça and tart, limey undertones. Winston Churchill said that "rugby is a hooligan's game played by gentlemen." While drinking the Southern Hemisphere, you're always going to feel like the latter.

National rugby pride can take many forms; in South Africa, it's exemplified in the Springbokkie, a shooter consisting of a creamy layer of Amarula—a local liqueur made from the fruit of the African marula tree—on top of a crème de menthe base. Named for the country's national animal, the springbok, and the South African national rugby team, the Springboks, the minty, fruity drink also has a gold and green hue to reflect the team's jersey colors.

SOUTHERN HEMISPHERE

MAKES 1 DRINK

1½ ounces pisco
½ ounce cachaça
¾ ounce fresh lime juice
¾ ounce simple syrup (see page 13)
6 mint leaves

Combine the pisco, cachaça, lime juice, simple syrup, and 5 mint leaves in an ice-filled shaker. Shake vigorously for 15 seconds and strain into a coupe. Perch the remaining mint leaf on top of the cocktail.

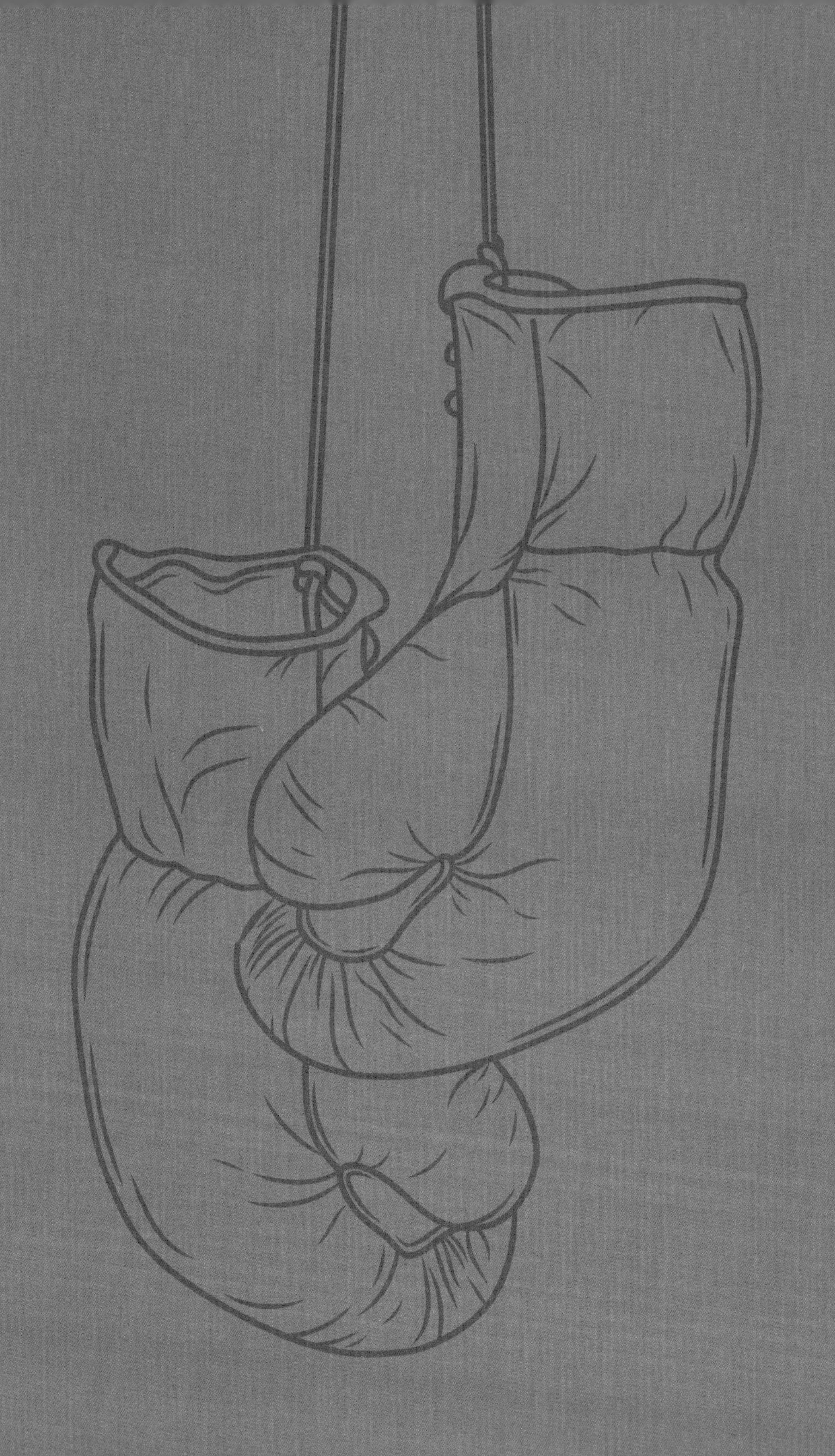

COMBAT SPORTS

WORLD HEAVYWEIGHT CHAMPIONSHIP (BOXING)

Muhammad Ali vs. George Foreman. Lennox Lewis vs. Evander Holyfield. Mike Tyson vs. Buster Douglas. Tyson Fury vs. Deontay Wilder. Considered to be among the greatest boxing matches of all time, one thing these legendary bouts have in common is that the winners either claimed or retained the much-coveted heavyweight title. The World Heavyweight Championship is the highest peak in professional boxing for fighters weighing more than 200 pounds, contested by some of the largest and most mythical figures in the sport's history, a remarkable gauntlet of physical prowess, resilience, and strategic acumen. While all four of boxing's major sanctioning organizations bestow titles (and recognize each other's legitimacy), since 1963, fights sanctioned by the World Boxing Council (WBC) have been considered the most illustrious, with the green-and-gold WBC Heavyweight Championship belt representing an unequaled legacy of excellence.

However, boxing fans were watching massive men with title aspirations batter each other in the ring long before the formation of the WBC, including the iconic championship duel between American Joe Louis and Nazi Germany's Max Schmeling in 1938, a powerfully symbolic victory for both African American athletes and democracy. That was the same era when Havana, Cuba's Floridita bar was in its heyday. Owned by boxing fanatic Constantino Ribalaigua Vert—a pal of amateur sparrer and professional drinker Ernest Hemingway—the hallowed watering hole served up countless rum-based classics like the pugilist-inspired Golden Glove. A hybrid of the daiquiri and margarita, as well as a spin on Ribalaigua's orange-tinged Daiquiri No. 2, this breezy, pleasantly dry, and citrusy punch to the taste buds will have you feeling as nimble as a prizefighter in his prime. And with only three ingredients, you'll be able to fix one faster than the break between rounds in a title fight.

The notoriously self-delusional Ernest Hemingway once asked Jack Dempsey, world heavyweight champion from 1919 to 1926, to spar with him during a trip to Paris in the mid-1920s. Dempsey declined, later saying, "I had this sense that Hemingway, who really thought he could box, would come out of the corner like a madman. To stop him, I would have to hurt him badly; I didn't want to do that." It's a good thing he didn't, otherwise we may never have gotten Hemingway's later literary masterpieces like *A Farewell to Arms* (1929), or the classic cocktails ascribed to him such as the Hemingway Daiquiri and the Death in the Afternoon.

GOLDEN GLOVE

MAKES 1 DRINK

2 ounces white rum
½ ounce Cointreau
½ ounce fresh lime juice
1 lime half-wheel, for garnish

Combine the rum, Cointreau, and lime juice in an ice-filled shaker. Shake vigorously for 15 seconds and strain into a double rocks glass that has been filled two-thirds of the way with crushed ice. Add a straw and top with more ice. Place the lime half-wheel in the glass alongside the ice.

UFC TITLE FIGHT

For the most part, twentieth-century practitioners of combat sports like judo, Brazilian jiujitsu, Muay Thai, and boxing kept to themselves. Sure, there was some crossover, such as Bruce Lee developing his own hybrid martial arts style in the 1960s and Muhammad Ali throwing down with Japanese wrestler Antonio Inoki in a 1976 exhibition. But it wasn't until the 1990s that mixed martial arts (MMA)—a no-holds-barred fighting sport incorporating techniques from dozens of older disciplines—was legitimized, thanks in large part to the founding of the Ultimate Fighting Championship (UFC) promotion company. Today, highly popular UFC Title Fights are some of the most fascinating spectacles in athletics, featuring the crème de la crème of male and female fighters in various weight classes, each bringing a unique blend of strengths into the Octagon, UFC's signature chain-linked ring. Divided into five-minute rounds, the action is equally brutal and strategic, measured and frighteningly impulsive, and at its best, a beautifully intense love letter to combat and a culmination of centuries of body-on-body warfare.

Every UFC fighter has a preferred prefight or postfight beverage, usually something caffeine- and electrolyte-rich to stay hydrated, but there are some extreme exceptions. Like Ilia Topuria, who downs half a liter of red wine the night before a bout. Or Tai Tuivasa having a "shoey" (chugging booze from a shoe) after a win. Then there's Lyoto Machida, who allegedly drinks his own urine, not just during the week of a fight, but on most days. The idea is that it helps to flush out his system more effectively, something that no scientist has ever felt the need to test.

An MMA fighter who grew up immersed in Brazilian jiujitsu will have a much different approach in the ring than, say, one who originally trained in capoeira. But there are universally effective maneuvers that have transcended many martial arts disciplines, like the chokehold, a submission move that critically reduces the air flowing through an opponent's neck to their brain. Less violently, it forms part of the pun in the Artichoke Hold, an unexpected and playful mai tai riff from New York bartender Jeremy Oertel. Emboldened by a plethora of complex flavors, the icy quaff is the liquid personification of an MMA fighter's stylistic experimentation, skillfully combining the unique bitterness of artichoke-based Cynar with spicy, funky, floral, and nutty elements for a roundhouse kick of cocktail bliss.

ARTICHOKE HOLD

MAKES 1 DRINK

¾ ounce Jamaican rum, preferably Smith & Cross
¾ ounce Cynar
¾ ounce fresh lime juice
½ ounce elderflower liqueur
½ ounce orgeat
1 sprig mint, for garnish

Combine the rum, Cynar, lime juice, elderflower liqueur, and orgeat in a shaker. Add 1 or 2 ice pebbles, shake for 5 seconds, and strain into a double rocks glass that has been filled two-thirds of the way with crushed ice. Add a straw and top with more ice. Place the mint sprig on top of the ice.

WORLD WUSHU CHAMPIONSHIPS

According to legendary actor, stuntman, and martial artist Jackie Chan, "Kung fu lives in everything we do." That total commitment to Chinese martial arts, also known as wushu, is perhaps most evident at the biennial World Wushu Championships, the sport-slash-lifestyle's signature event, bringing together the best practitioners from around the globe to showcase their skills. Competing in both choreographed individual routines called taolu ("forms") and Sanda, a combat sport that utilizes taolu techniques and includes elements of kickboxing and wrestling, athletes demonstrate their mastery of speed, power, and precision, as well as their artistic expression through fluid, dynamic movements. The competition, inaugurated in 1991 by the International Wushu Organization and held in widespread locales from Macao to Brazil, highlights the depth, diversity, and evolution of martial arts both in China and around the world.

The on-screen exploits of larger-than-life figures like Chan, Bruce Lee, and Chuck Norris have ensured that wushu occupies a prominent place, not just in sporting arenas, but squarely in the global consciousness, with its techniques and philosophies appearing in countless films and TV shows over the years. Including Quentin Tarantino's two-part epic homage to martial arts, *Kill Bill*, in which the protagonist uses an (apparently) fictional and very deadly wushu maneuver called the Five Point Palm Exploding Heart Technique. Which is also the name of a killer cocktail from mixological master Erick Castro, a bold, high-flying mixture of smoky mezcal, a slightly bitter Italian vermouth, and coffee liqueur. Despite its foreboding name, this darkly bold blend won't cause any immediate bodily harm, though its caffeine content, intense flavors, and unusual aromatics may cause your pulse to quicken—in a good way. A direct punch to the senses that would be cause for any wushu-minded cocktail nerd to bow in reverence.

Booze and wushu might not seem like a great combination, but for practitioners of drunken boxing or *zui quan*, the two are inseparable. Considered the hardest style of wushu to learn and requiring extraordinary balance and coordination, it's a series of techniques that imitate the falling and swaying movements of a drunkard, meant to trick your opponent into thinking you're inebriated.

FIVE POINT PALM EXPLODING HEART TECHNIQUE

MAKES 1 DRINK

1½ ounces mezcal
¾ ounce Punt e Mes (Italian vermouth)
½ ounce coffee liqueur
1 dash chocolate bitters, such as Scrappy's Chocolate Bitters

Combine all ingredients in a double rocks glass. Add ice and stir with a long-handled spoon for 5 or 6 seconds.

GRAND SUMO TOURNAMENT

Those unfamiliar with Japanese history might find sumo—which, at first glance, appears to be a brief contest where two overweight, thong-clad grapplers try to shove each other out of a small ring—to be an odd choice for a country's national sport. On the contrary, this highly ritualized and ancient martial art, inextricably linked to Japan's cultural identity for more than 1,500 years, requires years of strength-building, technical training, and a deep knowledge of Shinto religious practices from its wrestlers, the best of whom (called *yokozuna* or "grandmasters") showcase their skills in the annual Grand Sumo Tournament.

Also known as honbasho, this six-part competition starts in January and is held every other month in a different Japanese city for fifteen consecutive days. Individual matches start early in the morning and continue straight through until the early evening, when *makuuchi*, or high-ranking wrestlers, enter the ring (*dohyo*) and the excitement reaches its apex. Like any major sporting event, the Grand Sumo Tournament is a massive spectacle that goes far beyond wrestling. It's also a pageant of traditional kimonos and distinctive topknot hairstyles, intricately choreographed pre- and post-bout rituals, and unique food options like *chanko nabe*, a protein-packed stew of meat, fish, and vegetables that sumo wrestlers—who often weigh more than 300 pounds—consume daily.

But that's far from the only source of nourishment in the competitors' 20,000-calorie-a-day diets. For centuries, sumo wrestlers have been famous for regularly gulping down heroic quantities of beer and sake, Japan's national beverage. This fermented rice wine is also the base spirit in the Sumo in a Sidecar, an unexpectedly delightful reinterpretation of the classic. Nutty, fruity, and floral, traditionally balanced and decidedly modern, it's the perfect citrusy sidekick for a long day of Yokozuna-level indulgence, or just a solitary nightcap.

Legendary sumo wrestler Musashimaru Kōyō attributed his success to drinking beer every day. Specifically, the American Samoa–born Yokozuna would consume six pints during his 10,000-calorie lunch, which he said not only cooled him down, but also made him sleepy enough for a metabolism-slowing nap, adding girth to his already prodigious frame.

SUMO IN A SIDECAR

MAKES 1 DRINK

2 ounces sake
1 ounce apricot brandy
½ ounce fresh lemon juice
1 orange twist, for garnish

Combine the sake, apricot brandy, and lemon juice in an ice-filled shaker. Shake vigorously for 15 seconds and strain into a coupe. Rub the orange twist around the rim of the glass, peel side down, then place it in the glass.

WRESTLEMANIA

Professional wrestling's "Grandest Stage of Them All," WrestleMania is the sport's preeminent spandex-clad pageant, a convergence of pyrotechnics, elaborate entrances, and unforgettable high-flying moments, where legendary rivalries spawn climactic confrontations in front of millions, both live and worldwide on pay-per-view. Conceived in 1985 by Vince McMahon, then executive chairman of the World Wrestling Federation (now WWE), it's been the company's flagship annual event since its first edition in Madison Square Garden, where legends Hulk Hogan and Mr. T won the tag-team main bout. Since then, WrestleMania has been a must-watch hodgepodge of storytelling, outrageous celebrity cameos, and brawny showmanship from WWE Hall-of-Famers like The Undertaker, Ric Flair, Shawn Michaels, and Hogan, whose body slam of the 7-foot-4, 520-pound André "the Giant" Roussimoff at WrestleMania 3 is still considered one of the greatest athletic feats of all time.

Much of the action in the WWE may be scripted and some moves look, shall we say, slightly less than realistic. But wrestling is one of the most physically punishing professions, requiring a superhuman amount of strength and skill from its competitors, many of whom were standout athletes in other sports. Like "Stone Cold" Steve Austin, a former college footballer who headlined four WrestleManias. Reaching the pinnacle of the sport, Austin was famous for his brash, anti-establishment persona, as well as his "Stone Cold Stunner" finishing move and beer-chugging ability. If you're looking for something a bit more refined than light lager while taking in the WrestleMania drama, try the Stone Cold Fence. A jacked-up descendant of the Stone Fence—a combination of bourbon and apple cider considered to be America's oldest proto-cocktail—this bad boy is embellished with a jolt of coffee liqueur, citrus, and suds-free froth. A veritable cage match of flavor and texture that, like a devastating takedown by your favorite wrestler, will never leave you unsatisfied.

In addition to his otherworldly size and strength, three-time Wrestle-Mania participant André the Giant was also famous for his superhuman ability to imbibe vast amounts of alcohol that would kill the average drinker several times over. The booze-loving Frenchman would routinely down several bottles of wine before stepping into the ring and drink a minimum of twenty-four beers after competing, none of which seemed to have any effect on him. One of the rare instances where André actually appeared tipsy came after an epic night with fellow wrestlers Dusty Rhodes and Mike Graham in the 1980s, where he was said to have consumed 156 beers in a single sitting.

STONE COLD FENCE

MAKES 1 DRINK

1½ ounces bourbon
¾ ounce Mr. Black cold brew liqueur
½ ounce apple cider
½ ounce fresh lemon juice
½ ounce simple syrup (see page 13)
1 egg white
Club soda, to top

Combine the bourbon, Mr. Black, apple cider, lemon juice, simple syrup, and egg white in a shaker. Briefly shake without ice (to emulsify the egg white) for 5 seconds, then add ice and shake vigorously for 15 seconds. Strain into an ice-filled Collins glass. Top with club soda.

MOTORSPORTS

MONACO GRAND PRIX (FORMULA ONE)

The Monaco Grand Prix, one of the most prestigious events in the world of motorsport, is often described as the crown jewel of the Formula One (F1) calendar. It's an apt nickname for a race held in the heart of a swanky seaside principality, where glamour and opulence are a way of life, celebrity sightings are the norm, and spectators are just as likely to watch the proceedings from their private yachts as from the stands. It's not all lavishness and parties, however. The iconic racecourse, which has remained largely unchanged since 1929, is arguably the most challenging track in F1, a winding cityscape of narrow streets, tight turns, and zero room for error. But for those who survive to hoist the coveted, Louis Vuitton–designed trophy—and enjoy all the pomp that comes with it—the risk is more than worth the reward.

Formula One isn't just the biggest stage for the planet's finest drivers. It's also a technological showcase for the racing divisions of luxury auto manufacturers like Italy's Scuderia Ferrari. Far and away the most successful F1 team by total Grand Prix wins, Ferrari's cars have blasted off to numerous victories at the Monaco Grand Prix, thanks to gutsy performances by legends like Michael Schumacher, who won the race in 1997, 1999, and 2001. It's also the namesake of a cocktail made with equal parts Campari and Fernet-Branca, two beloved Italian amari that are as iconic as Ferrari's gold-and-black "prancing horse" logo. The intensely flavorful marriage of Campari's prominent bitter citrus notes and Fernet's forebodingly herbaceous qualities creates as overpowering a feast for the palate as Monaco is to the eyes. Balanced enough for slow sipping, it's often taken as a shot by industry professionals who know that in bartending, like F1, speed is paramount.

As part of one of the liveliest F1 traditions, the winner of the Monaco Grand Prix, as well as the drivers who finish second and third, pop bottles of sparkling wine on the podium and spray them all over one another. The practice dates to 1950, when Argentine Juan Manuel Fangio captured the French Grand Prix and was awarded a bottle of Moët & Chandon Champagne. At Monaco, however, the winning driver must clean up from their bubbly shower relatively quickly, as part of the prize includes dining with the country's monarch and his family the night after the race.

FERRARI COCKTAIL

MAKES 1 DRINK

1½ ounces Fernet-Branca
1½ ounces Campari

Combine both ingredients in an ice-filled mixing glass. Stir with a long-handled spoon for 25 to 30 seconds and strain into a coupe.

ISLE OF MAN TT

The Isle of Man, a self-governing British isle in the Irish Sea, is a quiet and picturesque, relaxation-friendly spot for most of the year. That feeling of serenity vanishes, drastically, for two weeks starting in late May, when the Isle of Man Tourist Trophy races dominate the island's landscape and many of its roadways. Founded in 1907, the TT, as it's commonly known, is the largest motorcycle racing event in the world, attended by more than 40,000 fans cheering on the sport's best riders as they attempt to survive the ultra-precarious Snaefell Mountain Course, a 37.73-mile circuit of sharp urban streets, rural public roads, twisting forested lanes, and treacherous mountain passes. Survival is indeed the operative word at what's been called the world's deadliest sporting event, where hundreds of participants, officials, and spectators have perished, and where at least one fatality per year is commonplace, to say nothing of the countless injuries.

Despite the risks, there are no shortage of motorcyclists clamoring to rip around the Snaefell Mountain Course, competing in several different classes based on engine size and overall machine weight. The most distinctive of these is the Sidecar TT, a fan-favorite event in which two-person teams—consisting of a driver and passenger riding in a motorcycle-with-sidecar—must navigate the course in perfect harmony. A similar, liquid form of kinship emerged in the early 1920s, when the cycling-inspired sidecar, a perfectly proportioned blend of brandy, lemon, and Cointreau, first appeared on drink menus in London and Paris. One of its earliest variations, the Chelsea Sidecar, substitutes the original base spirit for dry gin, which has lately begun to be produced at several Isle of Man distilleries. Sharp, vibrant, and botanical-rich, this Sidecar provides an elite race-day pick-me-up, preferably enjoyed at a safe distance from the course.

If you're looking to experience the flavors of the Isle of Man without subjecting yourself to potential bodily harm, buying a bottle of the local gin may be just the ticket, as the juniper berries used to make it are hand-foraged on the island. It's a lovely taste of the Manx terroir that won't involve eating pavement to avoid a crashing motorcycle.

CHELSEA SIDECAR

MAKES 1 DRINK

1½ ounces Manx dry gin, such as Fynoderee
¾ ounce Cointreau
¾ ounce fresh lemon juice
¼ ounce simple syrup (see page 13)

Combine all ingredients in an ice-filled shaker. Shake vigorously for 15 seconds and strain into a coupe.

24
AXALTA
24
AXALTA

DAYTONA 500

In the United States, motorsport begins and ends with NASCAR. The world's highest-ranked professional stock-car circuit, its normal race weekends regularly attract crowds in the hundreds of thousands (and more at the tailgates), with top drivers approaching demigod status for legions of fans. Yet that's nothing compared to the glory of winning the Daytona 500, NASCAR's most illustrious prize, which not only comes with exponentially more adoration, a substantial payday, and the coveted Harley J. Earl Trophy, but drivers also get to witness their car enshrined in the nearby Motorsports Hall of Fame of America for a year. That's how much this 500-mile, 200-lap thriller means to those lucky enough to score a ticket to Daytona International Speedway and the countless more who pack Daytona's beaches and byways every February, hoping to catch a small piece of the action. And between the deafening roar of the crowds, traditional flyovers by fighter jets, endless live music and food options, and the irresistibly rowdy atmosphere permeating every aspect of "America's Great Race," there's plenty to go around.

Even if you can't get the time off to snowbird your way down to Florida for a weekend in the sun, you would be remiss not to celebrate the Daytona 500—an unofficial national holiday in certain circles—without partaking in a beverage or . . . many. Instead of kneeling at the altar of Budweiser and Coors (where you certainly wouldn't be alone), elevate your game, at least temporarily, with a locally inspired favorite like the Daytona Daydream. This Floridian fantasy has an uncanny knack for satiating tropically inclined taste buds, thanks to a heaping helping of citrus, lots of buccaneer-approved spiced rum, and a creamy, coconut-centric finish. With only four ingredients, it's gleefully easy to make, so you won't miss any of the action at America's most famous track.

Daytona International Speedway is BYOB, so in case you want to make your life easy, you can leave the cocktails at home: The official beverage of the Daytona 500 is beer, specifically domestic, or, as of 2025, "American" brews from the Anheuser-Busch Company. Anyone caught sipping on fancier fare can face severe ridicule from their fellow patriotically inclined, suds-loving NASCAR fanatics.

DAYTONA DAYDREAM

MAKES 1 DRINK

2½ ounces fresh grapefruit juice
2 ounces spiced rum
1½ ounces coconut cream, such as Coco López
½ ounce pomegranate syrup (see page 13)
1 lime wedge, for garnish

Fill a tall glass with cracked ice and set aside. Combine the grapefruit juice, spiced rum, coconut cream, and pomegranate syrup in an ice-filled shaker. Shake vigorously for 15 seconds and strain into the glass. Perch the lime wedge on the rim of the glass.

50
50

24 HOURS OF LE MANS

In most sports, stamina and speed are often mutually exclusive. That's not the case in the 24 Hours of Le Mans, where drivers need a copious amount of both if they want to survive the oldest and most famous endurance-focused sports car race. Held in June at the notoriously dangerous Circuit de la Sarthe in Le Mans, France, the contest is unlike fixed-distance races in that the winner is the car—driven by multiple drivers in shifts—that covers the greatest distance in twenty-four hours. Beyond the countless gut-churning exploits on the course, Le Mans has become an epic arms race for rival auto manufacturers who constantly push the boundaries of innovation and performance, creating groundbreaking vehicles that are both miraculously durable and insanely fast. The extra layers of drama have been explored in highly regarded films like *Le Mans* and *Ford v Ferrari*, but to get the full picture, there's nothing like being there in person and hearing the engines roar in the summer heat.

Those lucky enough to experience Circuit de la Sarthe are treated to many unique track features, like the infamous Mulsanne Straight—where cars have reached speeds of 250 mph—and the Dunlop Bridge. The oldest of several footbridges sponsored by Dunlop Tyres at tracks around the world, it's the most recognizable landmark at Le Mans, located just before the Dunlop Corner, the first turn encountered by drivers after the start of the race. It also shares its name with a superbly appetizing rum and sherry amalgamation that appeared in Harry Craddock's *The Savoy Cocktail Book* (1930) and was probably being served during Circuit de la Sarthe's earliest days. Woodsy, herbaceous, and pleasantly dry, the decadent Dunlop Cocktail will have you going full throttle for a day at the track, or simply a nice dinner.

Although food stands are set up all around Circuit de la Sarthe, many fans attempt to sit in their seats for the entire twenty-four hours of the race. To accommodate this spectatorial test of endurance, race organizers allow ticket holders to bring their own food and drink, including booze, as long as it's not in glass containers.

DUNLOP COCKTAIL

MAKES 1 DRINK

2¼ ounces Caribbean blended rum, preferably aged 6 to 10 years
¾ ounce medium dry sherry, such as Amontillado
2 dashes Angostura bitters

Combine all ingredients in an ice-filled mixing glass. Stir with a long-handled spoon for 25 to 30 seconds and strain into a coupe.

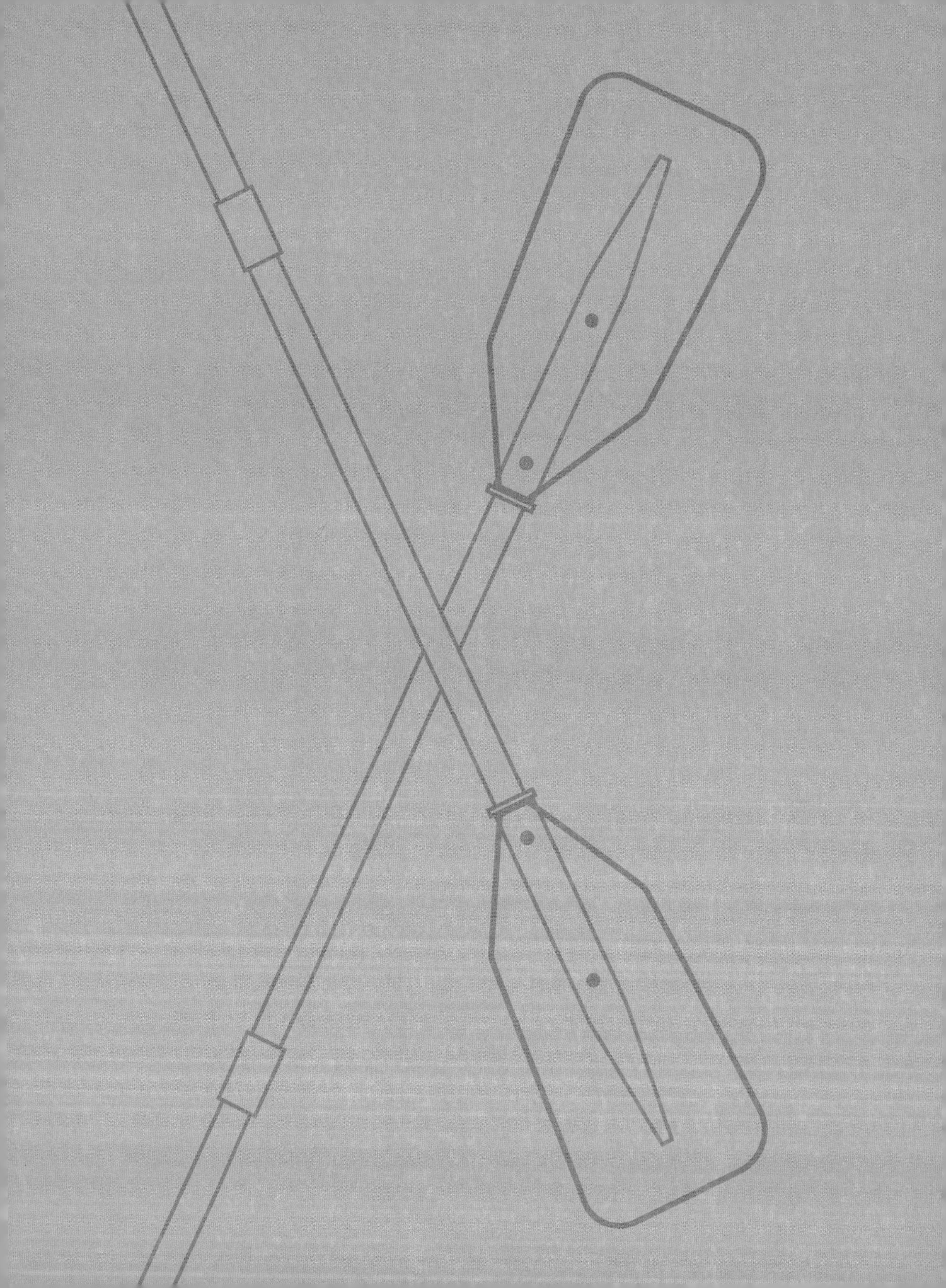

BOATS & ROWING

AMERICA'S CUP

As anyone in the yachting community will tell you, the America's Cup isn't just any sailing contest. In fact, it's the world's oldest international sporting competition, predating the modern Olympic games by forty-five years. First held in 1851 around the Isle of Wight off Southampton and Portsmouth in Hampshire, England, the race and its coveted trophy—also known as the Auld Mug—are named after its inaugural winner, the *America*, the flagship vessel of the New York Yacht Club (NYYC). Since then, it's been held every few years as a one-on-one match between the yacht club that currently holds the trophy versus a challenging club. With more than twenty victories, NYYC has had by far the most success, but clubs from the UK, Australia, New Zealand, and Europe—including landlocked Switzerland—have claimed the title in recent decades, making it a truly global affair and the most prestigious showcase for the world's best sailors and the sleekest, most technologically advanced, insanely expensive boats imaginable.

The 2017 edition of the America's Cup was held around Bermuda, one of the Atlantic's oldest and most distinguished yachting hot spots. And though the British territory's preeminent sailing organization, the Royal Bermuda Yacht Club, has yet to compete in the America's Cup, its namesake cocktail is in the upper echelon of nautical-themed beverages and one of the finest daiquiri variations you'll find on land or at sea. A Trader Vic original that first appeared in his 1947 *Bartender's Guide*, this dangerously easy-to-quaff rum and citrus beauty ratchets up the tropical, north-of-the-Caribbean vibes with almond-based falernum and orange curaçao. Classy enough to make drinkers of all stripes feel like they're cruising the waves in a $100 million sloop, you still might want to take it easy on these if you haven't got your barfly sea legs yet.

Unlike other famous trophies, the Auld Mug—which today is under constant supervision by its own security detail—has never been used as an actual drinking vessel. But similar vase-shaped jugs (also known as ewers) have been used to serve everything from water to wine since antiquity.

ROYAL BERMUDA YACHT CLUB

MAKES 1 DRINK

2 ounces gold rum, such as Gosling's
¾ ounce fresh lime juice
½ ounce falernum
¼ ounce dry curaçao
1 lime wheel, for garnish

Combine the rum, lime juice, falernum, and curaçao in an ice-filled shaker. Shake vigorously for 15 seconds and strain into a coupe. Skewer the lime wheel with a toothpick and perch it on the rim of the glass.

HENLEY ROYAL REGATTA

To earn a coveted spot on both the vaunted English social and sporting calendars is no easy task, but then again, nothing about the Henley Royal Regatta is common. Held every July on the Thames River near the town of Henley-on-Thames since 1839 (and patronized by the British monarch since 1851), it's the world's oldest and most highly regarded rowing event, the climax of the summer season, a blend of classic elegance, style, and top-notch athletics that's unlike any other competition. Offering six days of races on a 2,112-meter course, highlighted by the Grand Challenge Cup for men's Eights, the regatta was originally an amateur-only affair with strict rules about who could participate. However, after several controversies, including the banning of American rower John B. Kelly Sr. in 1920, and numerous accusations of classism, the event was finally opened to all qualifiers, regardless of status, in 1997, making the already fascinating and vibrant spectacle a true clash among the best of the best.

While some of the riverside vibes are decidedly upper crust, notably the ultra-exclusive Steward's Enclosure that's reserved for the organizers of the race and their posh guests, the regatta's fair-like atmosphere can be enjoyed by rowing fans of all social strata—provided they adhere to the garden-party dress code. Once vetted by the fashion police, attendees can gorge on traditional Henley provisions like tea sandwiches, strawberries, champagne, and Pimm's and lemonade, the event's favored tipple. For an elevated take on this summery English staple, try the Pimm's Fizz from Matthew Betts. Harnessing its namesake liqueur's herbal versatility and combining it with London dry gin, the drink offers a strikingly inclusive balance of sweet, sour, and spicy notes. And, with the addition of egg white, it froths up faster than the oar-churned Thames River during regatta week.

Pimm's and champagne may flow liberally at the Henley Regatta from sunup to well after sundown, but discerning event veterans traditionally start and end their day with another English on-the-water classic, the gin and tonic. Used for centuries by sailors to fend off malaria, the drink's anti-bloating properties (thanks to the quinine) make for perfect bookends to hours of rampant feasting and drinking.

PIMM'S FIZZ

MAKES 1 DRINK

1 ounce London dry gin, such as Beefeater
1 ounce Pimm's No. 1 liqueur
¾ ounce fresh lime juice
½ ounce pomegranate syrup (see page 13)
¼ ounce ginger syrup (see page 13)
1 egg white
Club soda, to top
2 to 3 fresh cranberries, for garnish

Combine the gin, Pimm's No. 1, lime juice, pomegranate syrup, ginger syrup, and egg white in a shaker. Briefly shake without ice (to emulsify the egg white) for 5 seconds, then add ice and shake vigorously for 15 seconds. Strain into an ice-filled Collins glass and top with club soda. Skewer the cranberries with a toothpick and perch them on the rim of the glass.

THE OCEAN RACE

It's not uncommon for veteran sports fans to wax nostalgic about the days when athletes played for love of the game and not increasingly outrageous paychecks. That old-school passion still exists among the sailors who compete in the Ocean Race, a nine-month, 49,000-nautical-mile yacht race around the world, where the reward for winning is a proverbial pat on the back. Held every few years since 1973, the insanely arduous journey follows the path of nineteenth-century trade routes, through some of the planet's most treacherous waters, including the wind-blown Southern Ocean, where waves often reach 150 feet and wind gusts regularly top 80 miles per hour. Besides the elements, the international crews must battle extreme fatigue, sailing up to twenty days and nights between pit stops, while subsisting on meager freeze-dried rations and wearing the same sets of clothes for weeks at a time. Talk about a labor of love.

In an event where speed and efficiency are everything, it's safe to assume that Ocean Race crews aren't stowing any extra cases of booze on board. But if you're one of the approximately 2.5 million fans who visit the race's various stopover points or tune in to watch it—and want to show solidarity with a few dozen cocktail-starved sailors—you'd be remiss not to fix yourself a Bright & Windy. This lighter, clear-spirited cousin of the Dark 'n Stormy has a name that conjures ideal yachting conditions and accurately reflects its botanical-rich, tangy, and slightly spicy flavor profile. Whether you want to celebrate a new maritime milestone or experience the spray of a sun-swept ocean in beverage form, this one's sure to raise your sails. And, thankfully, you won't have to travel thousands of nautical miles to procure the ingredients to make one.

Today, nautical races are won with technological advances and science-backed strategy, but that doesn't mean sailors are no longer superstitious. For luck, new ships are still formally christened in a ceremony that involves breaking sacrificial bottles of champagne over their bows before they set sail, a practice that dates back millennia, when tipsy Romans, Greeks, and Egyptians would pour wine on their vessels to appease their gods and ensure safe travels for their seamen.

BRIGHT & WINDY

MAKES 1 DRINK

2 ounces London dry gin, such as Beefeater
¾ ounce ginger syrup (see page 13)
½ ounce fresh lime juice
Club soda, to top
1 lime wedge, for garnish

Combine the gin, ginger syrup, and lime juice in a shaker. Add 1 or 2 ice pebbles, shake for 5 seconds, and pour into an ice-filled Collins glass. Top with club soda. Perch the lime wedge on the rim of the glass.

DRAGON BOAT FESTIVAL

Where will you be on the fifth day of the fifth month of the Chinese lunar calendar? If you happen to be in China and/or are a fan of incredibly ancient rowing competitions that double as cultural events, the likeliest answer is the Dragon Boat Festival, or *Duanwujie*. Held on various bodies of water across the country for more than 2,000 years, the national holiday commemorates the life and death of the statesman Qu Yuan, who drowned in a tributary of Hunan's Xiang River. The sporting activity at the festival centers around dragon boat races, thrilling contests between teams of rowers in specially outfitted longboats, paddling in unison to the beat of drums. While they're an important showcase for a growing sport with international aspirations, the races, which symbolize the valiant efforts of the fishermen who rowed out in vain to rescue Qu Yuan, are only one part of this community-focused celebration. Also included are traditional activities like eating zongzi, good-luck-bringing rice dumplings wrapped in bamboo leaves, shared among family, friends, and even rival rowing teams.

Food isn't the only refreshment that's exchanged at the Dragon Boat Festival, where Xionghuang wine is the beverage of choice. This potent blend of Chinese liquor (baijiu) infused with powdered realgar, a yellow-orange arsenic sulfide mineral, was traditionally used as both a pesticide and an antidote against venom, disease, and malevolent spirits. If ingesting arsenic isn't your jam, even for warding off evil, the Dragon's Breath is a baijiu-forward delight with powerful ingredients that are known for both their healing properties and universal tastiness. Created by Michael Thurm at Berlin's Parker Bowles bar, this piquant, berry-red beauty expertly melds its fiery, grain-based spirit with ginger, honey, raspberry, and habanero for a palate-pounding worthy of its namesake, while retaining, like winning dragon boats, a harmonious balance.

Most Westerners may be unfamiliar with baijiu, but China's national liquor is believed to be the most popular spirit in the world, produced in approximately 10,000 local and regional distilleries. And while foreign booze is more accessible than ever to Chinese drinkers, baijiu still accounts for 99.5 percent of all liquor consumed in the country, thanks to its outsized role in the local culture.

DRAGON'S BREATH

MAKES 1 DRINK

2 ounces baijiu, such as Ming River Sichuan Baijiu
¾ ounce fresh lemon juice
½ ounce ginger syrup (see page 13)
1 heaping spoonful raspberry preserves
2 dashes habanero bitters
Pinch of Sichuan peppercorns, for garnish

Combine the baijiu, lemon juice, ginger syrup, raspberry preserves, and habanero bitters in an ice-filled shaker. Shake vigorously for 15 seconds and strain with a fine-mesh strainer into a double rocks glass filled with ice. Grind the Sichuan peppercorns over the top of the drink.

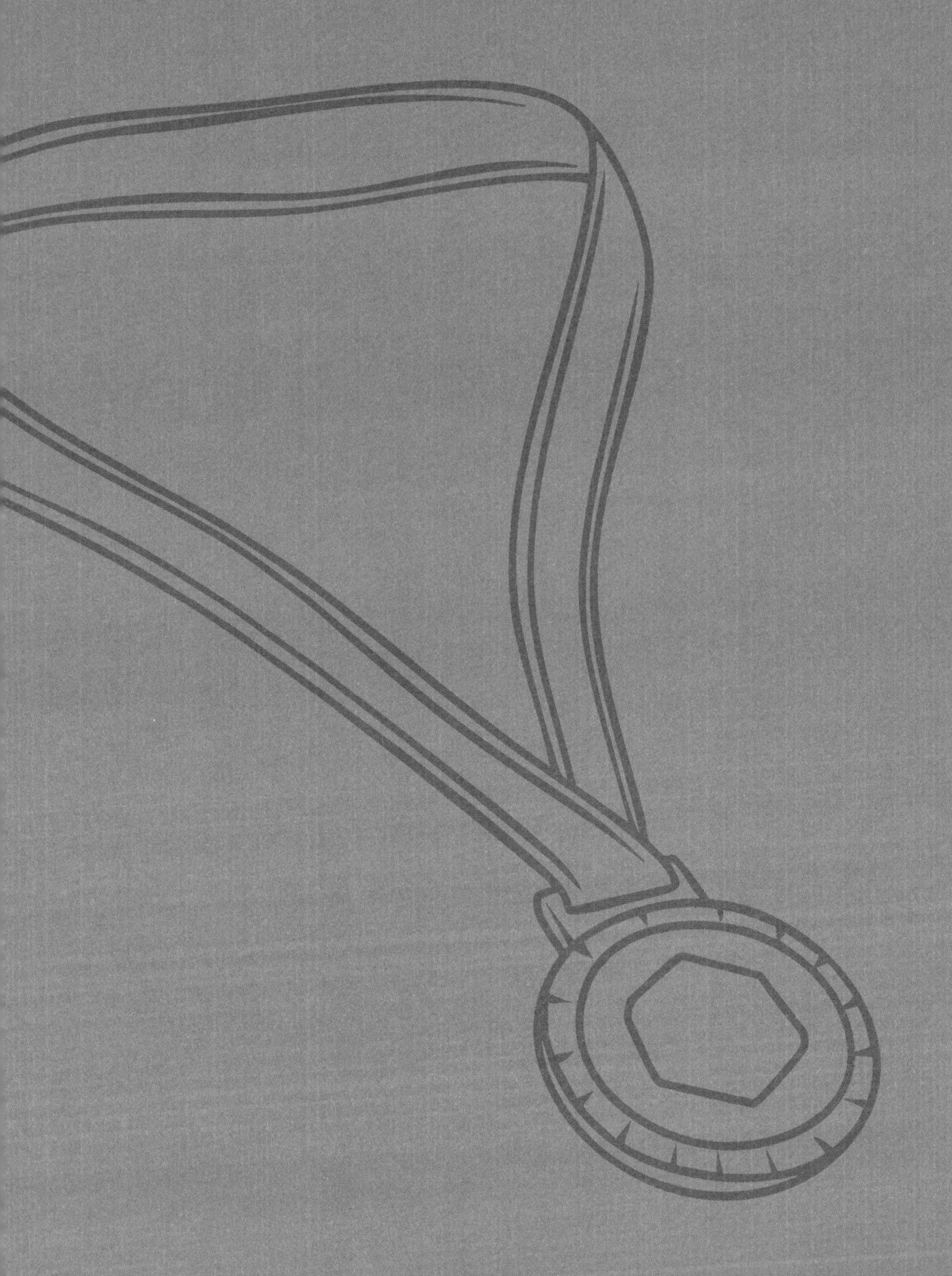

MULTISPORT

SUMMER OLYMPICS

It's safe to say that without ancient Greece, the world would be a vastly different place. Inventors of modern mathematics, sculpture, science, philosophy, and medicine, the Greeks were also responsible for the alarm clock, plumbing, and, in 776 BCE, the creation of the Olympic Games. Held every four years in honor of the god Zeus, these massively popular athletic and religious festivals were multisport showcases on a scale that wouldn't be seen again until 1896, when the first modern Summer Olympics took place in Athens.

Inspired by the ancients, the games were intended by the then-fledgling International Olympic Committee to be both a competition and a cultural exchange, where participating nations could put aside their differences in favor of unity and friendship. And while the planet's largest and most prestigious sporting experience has expanded greatly from 43 events and 14 participating nations in 1896 to 329 events and 206 countries in the 2024 edition, hosted games on five continents, and survived the rise and fall of empires and ideologies, doping scandals, and bomb threats, it's always stayed true to those original core principles. And that's something that would impress even the Greeks.

Unlike the ancient Olympics, where spectators would mostly drink wine and mead, the modern Summer Games were born during the Golden Age of cocktails, when drinks like the martini and Manhattan would go on to become as world-famous as the Olympics' most enduring symbols like the gold medal, the Olympic flame, and the Olympic flag with its interlocking rings. A slightly less heralded, yet no less fetching libation from the pre-Prohibition days is the Olympic Cocktail, which appeared in Harry Craddock's *Savoy Cocktail Book* (1930). Ostensibly inspired by the ocean liner the RMS *Olympic* (which was in turn named after the Games), this intriguing exploration of cognac and orange notes has the balance of a gymnast, the playful precision of a synchronized swimmer, and enough vitamin C to energize all manner of Olympians and the billions of fans who tune in to watch the competitions.

Most Olympics doping cases stem from the use of anabolic steroids or other designer performance enhancers. But the first person to have a medal stripped for a failed drug test at the Summer Games was under the influence of something far more innocuous: booze. At the 1968 Olympics in Mexico City, Swedish pentathlete Hans-Gunnar Liljenwall drank two beers to settle his nerves before the shooting portion of the event, after which he was immediately tested. Though Liljenwall would go on to win the gold medal, it was later taken away, making him the only athlete in Olympic history to be disqualified for drinking alcohol.

OLYMPIC COCKTAIL

MAKES 1 DRINK

1 ounce cognac
1 ounce dry curaçao
1 ounce fresh orange juice
2 dashes orange bitters
1 orange twist, for garnish

Combine the cognac, dry curaçao, orange juice, and orange bitters in an ice-filled shaker. Shake vigorously for 15 seconds and strain into a coupe. Rub the orange twist around the rim of the glass, peel side down, and place it in the glass.

WINTER OLYMPICS

For many outdoor enthusiasts, the arrival of cold weather is a truly frightful thing. For others, like the more than 2,000 athletes who compete every four years in the Winter Olympics, the appearance of snow and ice represents pure sports bliss. Founded in 1924 as a successor to Northern Europe's Nordic Games, the first global multisport competition featuring winter sports was held in Chamonix, France, and featured ski jumping, bobsledding, curling, ice hockey, skiing, and skating (figure skating and speed skating). These disciplines still form the core of the Games' more than one hundred events, testing the speed, agility, precision, and daring of the world's most cold-blooded competitors, while set against a backdrop of pristine peaks and icy-slick arenas. If high theater at the Northern Hemisphere's most spectacular locales (and sometimes outside of the venues, as anyone who remembers the Tanya Harding–Nancy Kerrigan incident can tell you), the Winter Games are the cherry on top of the proverbial snow cone.

From the "Miracle on Ice"—the United States men's hockey team's legendary upset of the Soviets in 1980—to Austrian skier Hermann Maier's terrifying seventy-mile-per-hour crash and subsequent gold medal performance in 1998, the Winter Olympics are no stranger to unforgettable moments. One of the unlikeliest occurred in Calgary in 1988 when a bobsled team from Jamaica made its debut. Though the four-man squad of former track stars crashed on their third run, their inspiring underdog journey was immortalized in the film *Cool Runnings*. An equally improbable yet highly intriguing combination of tropical vibes and cold-weather flavor can be found in the Winter Buck. It's a powerful liquid biathlon of funky Jamaican rum and warming allspice, supported by enough fresh ginger to keep the briskest of chills at bay. A perfectly jovial, full-bodied jolt after an epic day spent shredding on the snow or ice, or while on a Caribbean vacation, watching the Winter Olympics at a poolside bar

Nonalcoholic beer can be a divisive subject for both tipplers and teetotalers. But there's no doubt that the buzz-less brew has been a boon for the German Olympic team, who brought a thousand gallons of the stuff to the 2018 Winter Games in Pyeongchang, South Korea. According to the doctor of the German ski team, Johannes Scherr, nonalcoholic beer helps athletes recover more quickly, lowers inflammation, and contains high levels of antioxidants and immune-boosting polyphenols. Considering that Germany finished second in the overall medal count in 2018, he may be onto something.

WINTER BUCK

MAKES 1 DRINK

2 ounces Jamaican rum
¾ ounce ginger syrup (see page 13)
½ ounce allspice liqueur, such as St. Elizabeth Allspice Dram
½ ounce fresh lime juice
Club soda, to top
1 piece candied ginger, for garnish

Combine the rum, ginger syrup, allspice, and lime juice in a shaker. Add 1 or 2 ice pebbles, shake for 5 seconds, and pour into an ice-filled Collins glass. Top with club soda. Skewer the piece of candied ginger with toothpicks and perch it on the rim of the glass.

ASIAN GAMES

Stretching from the Mediterranean Sea to the Bering Strait, encompassing thousands of diverse languages, religions, cultures, and sporting traditions, Asia is an objectively massive place, any way you slice it. It should come as no surprise then, that the Asian Games, a quadrennial multisport competition founded in 1951, is the second-largest international event of its kind behind the Olympics. More than 12,000 participants from forty-five countries showcase the best of Asian athleticism in globally popular sports like track and field, swimming, and baseball, as well as regional, non-Olympic pastimes like sepak takraw, kabbadi, and wushu, and several games that organizers call "mind sports," including chess, bridge, and esports. Despite several boycotts, country bans, and other minor political squabbles during the Games' early decades, the event has persevered to become a unique melting pot of cultural heritage, camaraderie, and sporting excellence, one that truly lives up to its motto: "Ever Onward." For an area containing 30 percent of the world's landmass and 60 percent of its humans, that's no small achievement.

For decades, both Japan's best athletes and its finest whisky distillers have been lauded for their commitment to excellence. Those two passionate pursuits collide at the award-winning Ontake Distillery. Located in the Kagoshima Mountains, Ontake is the first distillery in the world to feature an on-site eighteen-hole golf course that's exclusively for cask owners, combining whisky and sport in a thrilling and unique way.

Designed by Indian artist K. K. Hebbar and inspired by the Olympic rings, the official symbol of the Asian Games is a rising sun with interlocking rings at its center, symbolizing hope, the promise of a new day, and unity among participating countries. That orb of positivity is also the inspiration for the Golden Sun, an Asian-centric take on Sam Ross's Sunflower. This stimulatingly floral medley utilizes whisky from multiyear host nation and frequent medal winner Japan (whose national flag depicts a similarly ascending celestial body), as well as arak, the traditional spirit of the Middle East, and mint, a major component in the cuisines of places like India, the location of the first Asian Games. Who knew that a liquid ode to unity could be this tasty?

GOLDEN SUN

MAKES 1 DRINK

¾ ounce Japanese whisky
¾ ounce elderflower liqueur
¾ ounce Cointreau
¾ ounce fresh lemon juice
1 barspoon arak
3 or 4 mint leaves

Combine all ingredients in an ice-filled shaker. Shake vigorously for 15 seconds and strain into a coupe.

X GAMES

For years, generations of extreme sports enthusiasts were relegated to the fringes of the athletic landscape, left to develop new skills and tricks in relative obscurity. That changed in a huge way in 1995 with the debut of the X Games, an annual, high-energy showcase backed by ESPN, which thrust sports like skateboarding, BMX, and motocross into the limelight like never before. First held in Rhode Island, the competition has turned unconventional superstars like Shaun White and Dave Mirra into household names, introduced adrenaline-pumping, action-sports terminology to a massive international audience, and jump-started a push by athletes to test the boundaries of what's humanly possible, a revolution that continues to this day. With the introduction of the companion Winter X Games in 1997, the festivities offer a year-round immersive spectator experience that, despite its brash branding, is also highly inclusive, fueling the exponential global growth of extreme sports in the twenty-first century.

X Games audiences have witnessed countless heart-stopping, career-defining, seemingly impossible accomplishments, perhaps none as seminal as skateboarding deity Tony Hawk completing the first 900—a two-and-a-half (900 degrees) aerial spin performed on a vert ramp—at X Games V on June 27, 1999. Similar ramps, also known as half-pipes due to their resemblance to cross-sections of large-diameter water pipes, are pervasive in all seasons, whenever a skater, BMXer, snowboarder, or skier wants to catch some serious air. That gravity-defying feeling is the inspiration for the Heaven in a Half-Pipe, a light and energetic tequila melange with enough spice—as well as plenty of vitamin C–heavy citrus and electrolyte-friendly cucumber—to put some bounce in your step (or board). Just make sure you shake up one of these complex and pleasantly potent potations *after* perfecting a new trick, not before.

More than any other extreme athlete, Tony Hawk has ridden his gravity-defying prowess to pop culture fame and entrepreneurial success, lending his name to skateboard companies, sneaker lines, and video games, while appearing in countless cameos and commercials. Recently, he's waded into the hospitality industry, partnering with acclaimed chef Andrew Bachelier to open Chick & Hawk, an Encinitas, California, eatery boasting upscale chicken sandwiches and a "killer" cocktail bar.

HEAVEN IN A HALF-PIPE

MAKES 1 DRINK

1½ ounces tequila
¾ ounce Ancho Reyes Verde Chile Poblano Liqueur
¾ ounce fresh lime juice
1 heaping spoonful pineapple preserves
5 thin cucumber slices
Pinch of cayenne pepper, for garnish

Combine the tequila, Ancho Reyes Verde, lime juice, pineapple preserves, and 3 cucumber slices in an ice-filled shaker. Shake vigorously for 15 seconds and strain into a coupe. Skewer the remaining 2 cucumber slices with toothpicks and perch them on the rim of the glass. Sprinkle with the cayenne pepper.

6
5
4
3

PARALYMPICS

The ability to overcome adversity—both the kind that's bestowed upon us at birth or after a life-altering tragedy—is one of the most remarkable human traits. Nowhere in sports is that more evident than in the Paralympic Games. This international, multisport competition is open to all disabled athletes and features a plethora of adapted or originally designed events as diverse and numerous as those in the Summer and Winter Olympics, which the Paralympics follows every four years. The games are the direct successor of the Stoke Mandeville Games, a gathering of British World War II veterans that was also called the International Wheelchair Games (whose main event, wheelchair basketball, is still a major draw). Today, as it continues to expand and transcend mere athletics, the Paralympics' mission, according to its website, remains the same: "to inspire individuals, bring about social change, and promote inclusive professional and sports opportunities for people with disabilities." That's something that all of us, able-bodied or otherwise, can get behind.

Intense competition and bitter rivalries are great, but sports are at their best when striving for unification, bringing people together for positive change that goes far beyond the results on the field—or pool, or court, or rink. Strength in togetherness is also the inspiration for the Unified Front cocktail. This tall, elegant crowd-pleaser combines ingredients from around the world—like the Paralympics, which hosts more than 4,000 athletes from 163 countries and federations—including spirits from Europe, vegetal elements from Asia, and a sweetener from North America. Fresh, citrusy, herbaceous, and fizzy, it's a shining example of the magic that can happen when distinctive flavors and textures come together for a single harmonious—and highly tasty—cause.

Some athletes might treat themselves to a glass of wine after an impressive performance or refuel with an electrolyte-replacement beverage. But not three-time Paralympic swimmer Mallory Weggemann, who, whether training or competing, would down a tall glass of chocolate milk after getting out of the pool. Often dismissed as a nostalgic treat from childhood, the calcium-rich drink contains a variety of nutrients essential for bone strength and rehydration, while providing an ideal balance of protein, fat, and carbs.

UNIFIED FRONT

MAKES 1 DRINK

1½ ounces gin
1 ounce fresh lime juice
½ ounce Suze
½ ounce agave nectar
5 thin cucumber slices
3 to 4 fresh Thai basil leaves
Club soda, to top

Combine the gin, lime juice, Suze, agave nectar, 3 cucumber slices, and Thai basil leaves in a shaker. Muddle briefly and add ice. Shake vigorously for 15 seconds and strain into an ice-filled Collins glass. Top with club soda. Skewer the remaining 2 cucumber slices with toothpicks and perch them on the rim of the glass.

MORE SPORTS

RUNNING OF THE BULLS—PAMPLONA

Success in most athletic activities is defined by achieving victory over one's competition. In bull-running, the goal is simply to make it out alive.

The adrenaline-fueled and controversial pastime of dashing in front of angry bulls that have been let loose on sectioned-off town streets originated in fourteenth-century Spain and continues, most famously, in Pamplona during the nine-day festival of San Fermin. Originating as a method for transporting bulls from the fields where they were bred to city markets or bullfighting rings, Pamplona's half-mile bull run, or *encierro* (as it's locally known), has become a massive tourist draw, attracting millions of visitors and dozens of thrill-seeking participants. Though lasting for only a few minutes, the exhilarating, often terror-inducing spectacle results in hundreds of injuries each year, as well as the occasional goring and death. Despite the danger, the event remains, in the eyes of the Spanish people, a testament to strength, courage, and the endurance of the human spirit in the face of adversity.

Some rules for bull runners at Pamplona specify that they must move in the same direction as the bulls, be at least eighteen years old, and not be under the influence of alcohol. But after bravely running alongside—and hopefully not being skewered by—a posse of massive, stampeding animals, you're going to want something to calm your nerves. The Bloody Bull is more than up to the task. Created at Brennan's, a popular breakfast and brunch spot in New Orleans, this bolder Bloody Mary cousin adds fortifying beef broth to the already spicy and savory mélange. The result is a forebodingly hued beverage that works equally well as a (slightly) nutritious post-run punch or for when you wake up feeling like you've been stabbed in the gut by a bull's horn.

A new, strictly enforced rule at Pamplona states that participants are not allowed to take selfies while running, which sounds like common sense, but it probably needs restating at an event where people risk getting spiked by cattle horns in the name of fun and logic has long been thrown out the window.

BLOODY BULL

MAKES 1 DRINK

2 ounces vodka
2 ounces tomato juice
½ ounce fresh lemon juice
1½ teaspoons beef broth concentrate, such as Swanson Beef Broth
3 dashes Worcestershire sauce
2 dashes Tabasco sauce
Pinch of kosher salt
Pinch of coarsely ground black pepper
1 lemon wedge, for garnish

Combine the vodka, tomato juice, lemon juice, beef broth concentrate, Worcestershire sauce, Tabasco sauce, salt, and pepper in an ice-filled shaker. Shake gently for about 10 seconds, or until the ingredients are well mixed. Strain into a Collins glass filled with cracked ice. Garnish with the lemon wedge.

CALGARY STAMPEDE

Encapsulating the traditions of rugged cowboy and cowgirl life, rodeos are a staple of the North American West. And while these breathtaking celebrations of herding-related athletics and community spirit are frequently associated with the United States, they're just as big in Canada's ranch-covered province of Alberta. And in the case of the Calgary Stampede, significantly bigger. With its origins dating back to 1884, "The Greatest Outdoor Show on Earth" welcomes more than one million visitors to the provincial capital every July for an electrifying ten days of classic rodeo competitions like bronco and bull riding, calf roping, barrel racing, and chuckwagon races, showcasing the agility, strength, and bravery of some of the grittiest cowpokes around. The atmosphere outside the arena is just as impressive, a sensory explosion of midways, agricultural and First Nations exhibits, pancake breakfasts, barbecues, and live music, highlighted by a massive opening-day parade, where even the staunchest of city slickers let out a few obligatory yee-haws.

Traditionally, the beverages most associated with ranching were whiskey and coffee, both of which you're sure to find in abundance at the Calgary Stampede. However, the event's many booze purveyors also offer a smorgasbord of local and international flavors, including choice spirits and brews from nearby distilleries and breweries, sophisticated cocktails from Calgary's chicest bars, and, of course, copious tequila shooters. Agave-based spirits are quite popular among cow-corallers (Ranch Water, anyone?) and have been since the first vaqueros were plying their trade in Mexico centuries ago. Their adventurous spirit is captured marvelously in the Rodeo cocktail, a product of the Austin, Texas, bar scene. This jacked-up cousin of the Tommy's margarita wrangles up notes of jalapeño-powered spice, citrus, and nectarous sweetness, tying them together nicely with a smoked-salt rim. Finish one and you'll be bucking like a bronco for a second round.

Enjoying a boozy breakfast at the Calgary Stampede was a longtime tradition for rodeo goers until the early 2000s, when some bureaucratic buzzkills decided to put an end to early-morning alcohol sales. That changed again in 2024, when the Alberta Gaming, Liquor & Cannabis Commission came to its senses and allowed bars and restaurants to start serving libations at 8:00 a.m. (and 7:00 a.m. on parade day).

RODEO

MAKES 1 DRINK

2 ounces mezcal
1 ounce fresh lime juice
½ ounce agave nectar
4 thin jalapeño slices

Combine the mezcal, lime juice, agave nectar, and 3 jalapeño slices in an ice-filled shaker. Shake vigorously for 15 seconds and strain into a double rocks glass filled with ice. Place the remaining jalapeño slice on top of the cocktail.

18

TOUR DE FRANCE

In 1903, when French journalist Géo Lefèvre concocted the idea of holding a five-part bicycle race as a scheme to boost sales of *L'Auto*, a daily sports newspaper, he could never have imagined what the Tour de France would become. Cycling's most admired (and grueling) annual spectacle, the approximately 2,200-mile-long modern version of the Tour has expanded to twenty-one full-day stages over twenty-three or twenty-four days, with teams of participants traversing just about every French landscape, from the Alps and Pyrenees to Paris's Champs-Élysées, where the race concludes each year but 2024, when, due to the Summer Olympics, the race finished up in Nice. It's also insanely popular. According to Tour organizers, roughly 3.5 billion people tune in to watch some of the world's best athletes compete for the coveted yellow jersey, which is donned before each stage by the rider with the lowest cumulative time.

Today's Tour de France cyclists are thought of as impeccably fit (and occasionally artificially enhanced) pedaling machines, but that wasn't always true. In the Tour's first decades, riders often shared cigarettes during the race—great for opening the lungs, apparently—and drank copious amounts of alcohol to numb their aching legs. One popular source of mid-race refreshment came courtesy of early Tour sponsor Bonal Gentiane-Quina, a fortifying herbal liqueur that was handed to weary cyclists by bottle-wielding company representatives. That earthy, spicy aperitif wears the metaphorical yellow jacket in Thomas Payne's Tour de France Cocktail, a fantastic spirit-forward boozer that features a trifecta of French flavors thanks to the additions of dry vermouth and Grand Marnier. Its relatively low alcohol content might give you ideas about taking a batch on your next bike ride, but trust us, this one's much better enjoyed with both feet planted firmly on the ground.

The Tour de France isn't just cycling's hardest race, it's also a great way to lose some excess booze weight. According to a recent study, the average cyclist burns between 4,000 to 5,000 calories during each stage of the race. That's nearly 124,000 calories for the entire Tour, which is the equivalent of drinking about 564 margaritas.

TOUR DE FRANCE COCKTAIL

MAKES 1 DRINK

1½ ounces French dry vermouth, such as Dolin
1 ounce Bonal Gentiane-Quina
¼ ounce Grand Marnier
2 dashes orange bitters

Combine all ingredients in a rocks glass. Add ice and stir with a long-handled spoon for 5 or 6 seconds.

MR. OLYMPIA

Arnold Schwarzenegger, arguably history's most famous bodybuilder and cinematic action hero, once quipped, "I just use my muscles as a conversation piece, like someone walking a cheetah down 42nd Street." Imagine how eye-popping it would be to behold not just one, but a couple dozen scantily clad, powerfully pulsing behemoths with impossibly sculpted physiques rivaling, or, in some rare cases, even exceeding that of the Terminator. That's the scene onstage at Mr. Olympia, the world's most prestigious bodybuilding competition, held every year since 1965, when Larry "The Legend" Scott flexed his way to the inaugural title. Since then, it's become a career-defining showcase for a who's-who of culturally iconic muscleheads like Lou Ferrigno, Franco Columbo, and Ronnie Coleman, whose eighth title in 2005 eclipsed Schwarzenegger's previous record total.

Bodybuilding as a professional sport is a relatively new phenomenon, but people have been ogling impressive anatomy way before the advent of spray tans and performance-enhancing "supplements." In ancient Greece, no name was more affiliated with being absolutely shredded than the mythological Adonis. A mortal man who was considered the peak of masculine beauty, he managed to beguile the goddesses Persephone and Aphrodite and eventually died in the latter's arms after being gored by a wild boar. Less tragically, he's also the inspiration for the Adonis cocktail. This easy-to-make yet charmingly nuanced mashup of Fino sherry and sweet vermouth was created at New York's Waldorf Astoria Hotel to celebrate the long-running Broadway musical of the same name, in which the titular hero, like a bodybuilder in all his or her glory, takes center stage. Bright, nutty, layered, and, unlike most other early martini-style cocktails, relatively low-proof, a couple of these powerfully flavored potations won't ruin your morning gym routine.

It's unclear when exactly the Adonis made its debut, but according to an 1887 article in New York newspaper *The Sun*, the drink was being sold that year in at least one downtown Manhattan bar with a mouthwatering price tag of 15 cents. Which, even adjusting for inflation, would be an absolute steal at any cocktail den today.

ADONIS

MAKES 1 DRINK

1½ ounces Fino sherry
1½ ounces sweet vermouth
2 dashes orange bitters
1 lemon twist, for garnish

Combine the sherry, vermouth, and orange bitters in an ice-filled mixing glass. Stir with a long-handled spoon for 25 to 30 seconds, then strain into a coupe. Rub the lemon twist around the rim of the glass, peel side down, then place it in the glass.

WORLD TENPIN BOWLING CHAMPIONSHIPS

College basketball coach John Calipari, defending his team after a loss, once told reporters, "You want perfection, go to a bowling alley!" He was likely referring to the act of bowling a 300, or a "perfect game," in which the bowler scores a strike—knocking down every pin—with each throw, as being a common occurrence. But while acts of bowling flawlessness do happen, that doesn't mean it's easy. In fact, as of 2025, there have only been forty-two perfect games in men's and women's competition at the World Tenpin Bowling Championships, the sport's most prestigious event, which was first held in 1954 in Helsinki, Finland. That's far from the only reason to tune into this epic, once-every-four-years battle of the best athletes from thirty-six countries competing for international supremacy in singles, doubles, team, and masters events, where the pressure and scores are mind-bogglingly elevated and where some of bowling's greatest legends are born. That's to say, it's a long way from your local alley.

If you're watching the WTBC, you'll probably hear the announcers mention the kingpin. In bowling, this refers to any pin that can make all the other pins fall when the ball knocks it down. It's also the name of the classic 1990s comedy in which Woody Harrelson's character, professional bowler Roy Munson, was quite fond of a postgame beverage. It's hard to have ill feelings toward the Kingpin cocktail, an early-twentieth-century classic that was originally made with Canadian whisky but is equally delightful when mixed using rye from south of the border. Notes of pineapple and lemon make this citrusy sipper an unbelievably easy-to-quaff refreshment, as smooth as a strike-seeking ball bowled down the center of the lane, and an amazing choice for celebrating a new high score, perfect or otherwise.

During the Prohibition era, the most popular form of bowling was called nine-pin. According to spirits writer Amber Thornton, the game was heavily associated with illicit activities, with many indoor bowling alleys doubling as prominent speakeasies. "To circumvent the Prohibition laws that came about to eliminate Nine Pin and its ties to gambling and drinking, players added a pin to the game and rebranded the sport as 'bowling,' thus creating the ten-pin game we know today."

KINGPIN

MAKES 1 DRINK

2 ounces rye whiskey or Crown Royal Canadian Whisky
1 ounce fresh pineapple juice
½ ounce fresh lemon juice
½ ounce simple syrup (see page 13)
Club soda, to top
1 lemon wedge, for garnish

Combine the rye, pineapple juice, lemon juice, and simple syrup in a shaker. Add 1 or 2 ice pebbles, shake for 5 seconds, then pour into an ice-filled Collins glass. Top with club soda. Perch the lemon wedge on the rim of the glass.

ARGENTINE OPEN POLO CHAMPIONSHIP

Polo is played in more than ninety countries, and few, if any, are crazier about the sport than Argentina, where horsemanship (or *gaucho* culture) has been a way of life for centuries. In a normal year, around 95 percent of the top-ranked polo players in the world hail from the South American nation and Argentinean pros who play for overseas clubs are known as "hired assassins." Unlike polo events in other places that are synonymous with elitism, Argentina's tournaments are massively attended, nationally televised displays of skill and passion, none bigger than the Argentine Open Polo Championship. Held at the Campo Argentino de Polo in Buenos Aires, "The Cathedral of Polo," since 1893, the annual competition pits eight of the best domestic clubs and two international squads against one another in fast-paced matches where bitter rivalries, heart-pounding final moments, and supreme athleticism—from both the players and specially bred polo ponies—conjure an excitement that's unparalleled in the sport, even for rabid Argentines.

When cooling off between the heated action on the fields, fans at the Campo Argentina de Polo can satisfy any gastronomical urge with an array of international favorites. However, the choicest refreshments skew local, especially where beverages are concerned. Regional white wines and Fernet and Cokes are always in vogue, but the most popular concoctions are gin and tonics mixed with maté, a bitter herbal tea made from the leaves of the yerba maté plant. That partnership of rich tea and juniper also permeates The Arriba, a spicy, sultry Last Word variation from David Tisue. There's a lot going on here, from the dry grassiness of the maté-infused gin to green Chartreuse's powerful botanicals, yet it still manages to be as balanced as a polo player winding up for a shot. One taste of this uniquely global yet authentically Argentinean refresher and you'll do anything—even commandeer a pony—to get another.

One of the many healthful properties of yerba maté is that it acts as a body tonic, with stronger natural antioxidant properties than traditional Chinese green tea. It's a great preparation tool for polo players and spectators alike, as well as a good hangover cure for the day after post-match polo parties and celebrations.

Recipe follows

THE ARRIBA

MAKES 1 DRINK

1½ ounces Yerba Maté-Infused Gin (recipe follows)
¾ ounce fresh lemon juice
½ ounce green Chartreuse
½ ounce agave nectar
1 lemon twist, for garnish

Combine the gin, lemon juice, green Chartreuse, and agave nectar in an ice-filled shaker. Shake vigorously for 15 seconds and strain into a coupe. Rub the lemon twist around the rim of the glass, peel side down, then place it in the glass.

Yerba Maté-Infused Gin

MAKES APPROXIMATELY 8 OUNCES

1 cup gin
2 tablespoons yerba maté

Pour the gin into a small container and stir in the yerba maté. Cover and let sit for 3 to 4 hours. Double strain the infused gin through a fine-mesh strainer and some cheesecloth or a paper towel into another container.

FIVB BEACH VOLLEYBALL WORLD CHAMPIONSHIPS

Like many beloved Olympic sports, professional beach volleyball tends to pop up on general sports fans' radars once every four years and then disappear once the medals have been handed out. Which is unfortunate, because the Fédération Internationale de Volleyball (FIVB), the governing body for the toughest game on bare feet, organizes dozens of equally intense tournaments at some of the swankiest, sun-soaked locales around the world. The pro tour's biggest, most beneficent, and best attended event is the double-gender FIVB Beach Volleyball World Championships, a raucous biennial bash where the top forty-eight teams in the international rankings battle it out for nine days, diving, spiking, and blocking their way to the sport's biggest prize pool and the unequaled honor of being crowned kings and queens of the sand.

From their impressively toned physiques, deep tans, scanty attire, and stylish sunglasses to the loud rock music and party atmosphere that surrounds them at tournaments, volleyball pros are some of the most effortlessly sexy athletes around. But if you've ever struggled to remove grit from bodily crevices you didn't know existed while soaking your aching muscles after a sweltering day on the courts, you understand that this punishing pastime is the farthest thing from a fun day near the water. To harness some truly relaxing seaside vibes, with or without the workout, get your hands on a Volley Colada, an exquisite après-volleyball indulgence adapted from a similar drink created at the *Make Me a Cocktail* website to celebrate the beach volleyball tournament at the 2024 Olympics. Blend up a few of these calorically impressive, cream-topped combos of coconut rum, passionfruit, pineapple, and mint at your next beachfront bonanza and you'll get louder applause than a soon-to-be world champion icing their opponent with a thunderous ace.

According to historians, the first beach volleyball game was played on Hawaii's Waikiki Beach by members of the Outrigger Canoe Club. Waikiki is also the birthplace of bartending legend Harry K. Yee, whose innovations like the Blue Hawaii, banana daiquiri, and garnishing drinks with paper parasols are just as much staples of beach culture as volleyball nets.

Recipe follows

VOLLEY COLADA

MAKES 1 DRINK

2 ounces coconut rum
1½ ounces fresh pineapple juice
¾ ounce passionfruit syrup
¼ ounce fresh lime juice
¼ ounce simple syrup (see page 13)
1 splash heavy cream
1 sprig mint, for garnish

Combine the coconut rum, pineapple juice, passionfruit syrup, lime juice, simple syrup, and heavy cream in a shaker. Add 1 or 2 ice pebbles, shake for 5 seconds, and pour into a tall glass or tiki mug filled two-thirds of the way with crushed ice. Add a straw and top with more ice. Place the mint sprig on top of the ice.

WORLD POOL CHAMPIONSHIP

Most barflies, and even casual inebriates, are familiar with pool, or have at least noted the ubiquitous thwack of balls and raucous cheers emanating from the green-cloth-covered tables found in pubs across the globe. In the United States, the version du jour is usually eight-ball pool, but international pros earn the highest notoriety and prize money in nine-ball—which involves pocketing nine colored billiard balls in ascending numerical order—the version played at the World Pool Championship. Founded in 1990 by the World Pool Association, the premier annual event on the cue sports calendar is famous for attracting the world's top talent for a fascinating show of strategy, technique, finesse, and perfect aim. Beyond the unbelievably high level of gameplay, the tournament is notable for its well-mannered audience, whose hushed anticipation only adds to the tension and exhilaration. Meaning, if you're planning on going, leave the rowdy pool hall behavior at the door.

Pool and drinking have always gone hand in hand, something known all too well to hosts who have spent hours cleaning circular stains off their home tables. Or bartenders who have listened to countless sob stories from customers about being hustled by pool sharks, cunning players who take monetary advantage of less skilled (or less sober) competition. The term can also simply refer to anyone who's exceptionally good at cue sports, which is the real inspiration for the Pool Shark Punch, a tall, tasty rum number that's guaranteed to lighten the vibes at pool-table milieus of all varieties, from the tidiest professional setups to the dingiest dives. With a hue nearly identical to the green felt that covers most tables, thanks to Midori and lime, this fizzy, tropically inclined stress-reliever goes down smoother than a perfectly placed eight ball into a corner pocket.

Unlike other pub-related sports, like darts, that have outlawed the consumption of alcohol during competitions, professional pool's governing bodies decided to remove booze from their banned substances list in 2018. Still, it's extremely rare to catch a pro pool player at any level sneaking a sip during a match.

POOL SHARK PUNCH

MAKES 1 DRINK

1½ ounces white rum
1½ ounces fresh pineapple juice
½ ounce fresh lime juice
¾ ounce Midori melon liqueur
½ ounce Cointreau
Club soda, to top
1 pineapple leaf, for garnish
1 pineapple wheel, for garnish

Combine the rum, juices, Midori, and Cointreau in a shaker. Add 1 or 2 ice pebbles, shake for 5 seconds, and pour into an ice-filled Collins glass. Top with club soda. Place the pineapple leaf in the glass beside the ice and perch the pineapple wheel on the rim of the glass.

20
1
18
4
13
6
10
15
2
7
16
11
14
9
12
5

PDC WORLD DARTS CHAMPIONSHIP

The local pub, ostensibly, is a haven of relaxation, a welcome escape from work, sobriety, and other trivialities of day-to-day life. But it's also a place where disagreements can flow faster than the pints, even among good friends. One such scuffle occurred in 1992 in the world of darts—the most popular pub game in Europe and North America since its emergence in 1860s England—when several disgruntled players quit the British Darts Organization (BDO) to form the Professional Darts Corporation (PDC). After years of vying for supremacy with the now-defunct BDO, the PDC is considered the highest level of competition in the sport today and hosts several tournaments each year, the most prestigious being the World Darts Championship, held at London's Alexandra Palace since 2008. It's a battle of the top thirty-two players in the world darts rankings, an additional thirty-two British pros, and thirty-two international qualifiers, with the winner hoisting the coveted Sid Waddell Trophy and being crowned world champion, no arguments allowed.

While darts and pub culture will always be intertwined, today's professional darts organizations emphasize skill and performance during tournaments. Alcohol hasn't been allowed onstage at televised events since 1989, but seasoned pros are still known to sneak a nerve-calming sip or two off camera.

Beer and darts have been bedfellows since the sport's earliest days, from the most casual dive bar matches to professional bouts. It was common in televised tournaments in the 1980s to behold chain-smoking pros of greatly varying physiques calming their nerves between throws with a glass or three. That love affair between darts and suds remains, even inspiring cocktails like the Bull's Eye. Named for the hard-to-hit center circle of a dartboard and originating in Cuba, this beer-based Moscow Mule variant is tough to beat when it comes to crisp, fizzy, and gingery refreshment. Though it probably won't have you hitting your spots with the accuracy of a dart-throwing superstar, it will certainly give you the confidence to try.

BULL'S EYE

MAKES 1 DRINK

½ ounce fresh lime juice
¾ ounce ginger syrup (see page 13)
½ ounce simple syrup (see page 13)
1 (12-ounce) can or bottle light beer, such as Modelo
1 lime wedge, for garnish

Combine the lime juice, ginger syrup, and simple syrup in a shaker. Add 1 or 2 ice pebbles, shake for 5 seconds, and pour into a pint glass that has been filled halfway with cracked ice. Top with the beer and stir for 5 seconds with a long-handled spoon. Perch the lime wedge on the rim of the glass.

WORLD'S STRONGEST WOMAN

Historically, female powerlifters, bodybuilders, and other strength-based athletes unfortunately have been overshadowed by their masculine counterparts. Early twentieth-century strongwomen like Abbye Stockton—famous for holding her husband above her head in adjoining handstands—were relegated to performing routines instead of proving themselves in competition. The emergence of female bodybuilding contests in the 1980s was a step toward equality, but it wasn't until the creation of the World's Strongest Woman in 1997 that the most powerful female athletes could put their muscles to the ultimate test against their buffest peers. A vibrant symbol of progress and empowerment, the event, held in wide-ranging locations from Kuala Lumpur to Daytona Beach, has been the scene of some astonishing feats, like Robin Coleman (aka "Helga" on *American Gladiators*) squatting a car fifteen times in 2001, or Aneta Florczyk—a world record holder for successively deadlifting twelve men—winning an unprecedented four consecutive titles in the mid-2000s.

Raw strength is obviously important in, um, strongwoman competitions, but endurance, skill, and determination are equally important attributes for championship contenders. Likewise, for highly potent cocktails to be drinkable for those who have left the frat basement scene behind (sorry, Jungle Juice), they must be balanced, at least partially nonabrasive, and possessed of an interesting flavor profile that's conducive to repeat sipping. The Aunt Roberta, frequently described as the world's deadliest cocktail, checks all the boxes. Created in Alabama in the 1800s by a traveling apothecary of the same name, this mélange of heavy-lifting brandy and absinthe alongside black raspberry liqueur, sweet vermouth, and bitters is not for the faint of liver. But beyond the diabolical alcohol content, this complex tapestry of botanicals and herbal notes can be a joy to experience in moderation. There's nothing casual about the World's Strongest Woman, and a drink toasting to it shouldn't be either.

The exact proportions of the ingredients in the Aunt Roberta tend to vary significantly, depending on who's making it. But all variations share one thing in common: They're super strong. Notably, one version found on the *Make Me a Cocktail* website boasts an alcohol content of nearly 39.5 percent, making it significantly stronger than the average cocktail, which ranges from 15 to 30 percent.

Recipe follows

AUNT ROBERTA

MAKES 1 DRINK

2 ounces cognac
¾ ounce sweet vermouth
½ ounce black raspberry liqueur, such as Chambord
½ ounce absinthe
2 dashes Angostura bitters
1 lemon twist, for garnish
1 brandied cherry, for garnish

Combine the cognac, vermouth, black raspberry liqueur, absinthe, and bitters in a double rocks glass. Add ice and stir with a long-handled spoon for 5 or 6 seconds. Rub the lemon twist around the rim of the glass, peel side down, then place it in the glass. Drop the brandied cherry into the glass.

WORLD'S STRONGEST MAN

Chances are you don't pull airplanes with your bare hands, lift tree-size logs over your head, or carry 900-pound refrigerators around an obstacle course for fun. That doesn't mean you can't enjoy watching the athletes competing in the World's Strongest Man tackle those feats, and many more that are equally as outrageous. And you wouldn't be alone. That was the idea that TV producers Douglas Webster and David Edmunds had when they pitched what would become the premiere international strongman competition to CBS in the late 1970s. The annual contest, originally dominated by former American football players and lifelong powerlifters, was an immediate hit with audiences, introducing them to gargantuan legends like Bill Kazmaier, who at one time held more than a dozen world records in events like bench press, stone block throw, and Hungarian farm cart deadlift. His feats, as well as subsequent performances by the likes of Icelandic icons Jón Páll Sigmarsson and Magnús Ver Magnússon, helped grow the event into a global phenomenon, averaging around 220 million viewers a year—proof that just about everyone loves a real-life superhuman power-fest.

Many of today's World's Strongest Man participants, rather than being former professional athletes in other sports, start training specifically as strongmen at an early age. Like Hafþór Júlíus Björnsson—another Icelander best known for portraying "The Mountain" Ser Gregor Clegane on *Game of Thrones*—who, at 6′9″ and 400 pounds, is widely considered to be one of the most powerful humans of all time. Getting enough energy to work out such a massive bodily machine probably requires a good jolt of coffee, one of the prominent flavors in the World's Strongest Man cocktail from Detroit bartender Beaux Kerin. Jacked up with herbaceous notes from Amaro Averna, its base spirit is black strap rum that's been mixed with half-and-half, frozen, and thawed through a filter, a process that does require a bit of metaphorical heavy lifting. But at least you won't have to raise a car to earn your friends' respect; just serve them a couple of these delightfully rich tipples.

World's Strongest Man athletes are known to have extreme lifestyles, and Eddie Hall, winner of the 2017 edition and former deadlift world-record holder, is no exception. Nicknamed "The Beast," the British-born strongman claimed in an interview that he would do whatever it took to get a good night's sleep before a competition, including downing an entire bottle of vodka, earning him the unofficial title of World's Strongest Liver.

Recipe follows

WORLD'S STRONGEST MAN

MAKES 1 DRINK

1½ ounces Milk-Washed Cruzan Black Strap Rum (recipe follows)
½ ounce Amaro Averna
½ ounce coffee liqueur, such as St. George NOLA

Combine all ingredients in an ice-filled shaker. Stir with a long-handled spoon for 25 to 30 seconds and strain into a coupe.

Milk-Washed Cruzan Black Strap Rum

MAKES ABOUT 10 OUNCES

10 ounces Cruzan Black Strap Rum
1 ounce half-and-half

In a freezer-safe container with a lid, combine all ingredients. Freeze until solid, about 4 hours. Place the mixture in a large Superbag filter over a large plastic container and allow the mixture to thaw. Once melted, the half-and-half-infused rum will have passed through the bag, leaving the milk solids behind.

USA PICKLEBALL NATIONAL CHAMPIONSHIP

For a seemingly innocuous and inclusive sport, pickleball sure does attract a lot of haters. Yet despite the myriad complaints—it's silly and not as "serious" as other racquet sports; pickleball courts often encroach upon or completely replace existing basketball and tennis courts; the hard plastic balls are annoyingly loud when hit—it's the fastest growing pastime in the United States and the official sport of the state of Washington, where it was invented as a children's backyard game in 1965.

Today, pickleball isn't just for recreational enthusiasts or aging ex-tennis players. The men and women of the Pro Pickleball Association (PPA) are formidable athletes, battling it out in intense competitions throughout the year, arguably the most prestigious of which is the U.S. Open Pickleball Championships, held every fall in Naples, Florida. In addition to the professional singles, doubles, and mixed doubles bouts, the weeklong shindig—attended by more than 30,000 spectators and participants—features casual matches, community events, and live entertainment and has been dubbed "the biggest pickleball party in the world."

Beverages tend to flow liberally at festivities of this magnitude, and with Margaritaville sponsoring the event since its inception in 2016, it's a safe bet to assume that the lifestyle brand founded by the late, great Jimmy Buffett provides copious amounts of its namesake libation to attendees and players alike. For an even more on-brand take on the agave-based classic, try the Pickle Brine Margarita from Brooklyn bartender Heather Rush. Salty, sweet, and spicy, with lush notes of umami (and plenty of electrolytes from the pickle juice), it's a delightfully customizable post-match quaff after an afternoon sweating it out on the courts or just taking in the action.

Capitalizing on the sport's exploding popularity, alcohol brands and hotels across the U.S. have begun offering "boozy pickleball experiences" to of-age players of all abilities. Like Carneros Resort and Spa in Napa Valley, California, which boasts two pickleball courts in collaboration with Veuve Clicquot Champagne, complemented by the Veuve Clicquot Champagne Bar & Lounge for postgame relaxation. Or Georgia's Chateau Elan Winery & Resort, which offers a wine and pickleball weekend that includes pickleball instruction and court time, along with wine tours and tastings.

PICKLE BRINE MARGARITA

MAKES 1 DRINK

1½ ounces tequila or mezcal
1 ounce pickle brine, preferably from classic dill pickles
1 ounce fresh lime juice
¾ ounce Cointreau
2 teaspoons granulated sugar
2 or 3 dashes habanero hot sauce (optional)
2 pickle chips, for garnish

Combine the tequila, pickle brine, lime juice, Cointreau, sugar, and hot sauce (if using) in an ice-filled shaker. Shake vigorously for 15 seconds and strain into a double rocks glass filled with ice. Skewer the pickle chips with toothpicks and perch them on the rim of the glass.

PIPE MASTERS

Of the hundreds of professional surfing contests around the globe, several claim to be the sport's biggest. And while Portugal's Nazaré Big Wave Challenge produces the most monstrous waves ever surfed (on the rare chance that conditions allow for it), there's no fiercer challenge for the ocean's top wave riders than the Pipe Masters. The final stop on the World Surf League (WSL) Championship Tour, featuring all the WSL's highest ranked male and female athletes, it's held at Oahu, Hawaii's Banzai Pipeline, famous for its powerful, barreling waves that are consistently considered the best in the world. With the WSL title at stake, the competition is as gnarly as the surf, a proving ground for up-and-comers and seemingly ageless legends like Kelly Slater, who's won the event a record eight times.

Ingenuity, creativity, and a knack for rolling with whatever nature throws at you are all vital attributes of a championship surfer. Those qualities are also inherent in the craftiest cocktail makers. Like certified mad scientist Eric "ET" Tecosky, a mainstay of the Los Angeles bar community, whose most diabolical concoction is, unquestionably, the Surfer on Acid. Debuting in the early 1990s, at a time when surf fashion and culture were bursting onto the mainstream cultural consciousness, this three-part slammer takes two relatively benign tiki ingredients, coconut rum and pineapple juice, and combines them with infamous German amaro Jägermeister. The somewhat intimidatingly sludge-colored result is shockingly enjoyable. A perfect pairing of bitter, fruity, and sweet notes, unabashedly strong but not overpoweringly so, it's the ultimate refreshment after a long day cruising the waves or when you're sitting at the bar dreaming about them.

It's never a good idea to go surfing after having a few cocktails, and that's especially true in South Korea, where, as of 2025, it's illegal to ride a surfboard with a blood alcohol content of 0.03 or higher, according to *The Korea Times*. Anyone found to be in violation of the law can face a fine of up to 1 million won (approximately $685 USD).

SURFER ON ACID

MAKES 1 DRINK

1 ounce Jägermeister
1 ounce coconut rum
1 ounce fresh pineapple juice
1 pineapple wedge, for garnish

Combine the Jägermeister, coconut rum, and pineapple juice in an ice-filled shaker. Shake vigorously for 15 seconds and strain over ice into a double rocks glass. Perch the pineapple wedge on the rim of the glass.

AMERICAN CORNHOLE LEAGUE WORLD CHAMPIONSHIP

For much of its history, cornhole—or "bags," as it's known in some parts of the United States—was seen as little more than a fun way to pass the time at fairs, frat parties, backyard barbecues, bar patios, and anywhere else that's conducive to tossing bean bags at wooden boards and having a chill time. That's changed in recent years with the creation of several organizations that have sought to standardize the rules of the game and turn it into a legitimate professional sport.

The most successful of these, the American Cornhole League (ACL), has operated since 2015 and hosts 25,000 amateur and pro tournaments each year, the pinnacle being the ACL World Championship. This ten-day, nationally televised extravaganza, featuring men's and women's singles and doubles and mixed doubles matches, attracts the world's best players, many of whom look like they've spent way too much time at the seediest of dive bars (and probably have). Yet make no mistake, these are remarkably skilled athletes, whose ability to regularly and accurately place their bags wherever they want on the board or in the hole is a truly jaw-dropping sight to behold.

Most sports discourage boozing while playing, but not cornhole. According to Cornhole Worldwide, one of the largest suppliers of cornhole boards and bags, moderate imbibing during a match is great for settling the nerves and improving concentration. Furthermore, holding a beer or cocktail creates the perfect counterweight in your off hand to help balance your throws.

Today, the bags used in top tournaments are usually filled with plastic resin or other synthetic materials that better maintain a consistent weight and shape during competitive play. But it's still possible to find ones filled with preserved corn kernels, just as they were during the game's early days in major corn-producing states like Indiana and Kentucky. The maize milieu also extends to the cocktail world, in corny concoctions like the Charred Corn Mezcalita. Earthy, smoky, salty, nutty, and citrusy, it's quite complex yet accessibly smooth, as satisfying as silencing your opponent with an impeccably placed cornhole toss.

Recipe follows

CHARRED CORN MEZCALITA

MAKES 1 DRINK

Kosher salt, for rimming glass
Lime wedge, for rimming glass
2 ounces mezcal
1 ounce fresh lime juice
½ ounce agave nectar
½ ounce Charred Corn Puree (recipe follows)
1 lime wedge, for garnish
1 sprig cilantro, for garnish

Spread some salt over a small plate. Run 1 lime wedge around the rim of a Collins glass, then dip the rim into the salt to coat. Combine the mezcal, lime juice, agave nectar, and charred corn puree in an ice-filled shaker. Shake vigorously for 15 seconds and strain over ice into the prepared glass. Place the lime wedge and cilantro sprig in the glass alongside the ice.

Charred Corn Puree

MAKES APPROXIMATELY 8 OUNCES

1 or 2 ears of corn, shucked

Grill or char the corn until slightly blackened. Let cool and remove the kernels from the cob(s). Transfer to a blender and process until smooth.

IRONMAN WORLD CHAMPIONSHIP

Attaining elite status in one endurance sport is impressive. To reach that level in three very different athletic disciplines is absolutely wild. Yet that's par for the course for the superhumans who travel to Kona, Hawaii, to take on the Ironman World Championship, an annual culmination of Ironman triathlon qualification races that consists of a 2.4-mile open-water swim, a 112-mile bike ride, and a full 26.2-mile marathon, for a total distance of 140.6 miles. The idea for the event was hatched by John and Judy Collins, a husband-and-wife triathlete duo who often mused about which long-distance athletes were the fittest—swimmers, runners, or cyclists—a question they first put to the test in 1978 (hint: they're all pretty damn fit). Since then, the Ironman has become an impressive symbol of strength, stamina, and mental toughness, an increasingly popular spectacle that's hosted countless inspiring moments. Like college student Julie Moss collapsing near the finish line in 1982 and subsequently crawling the rest of the way. Or disabled athlete John MacLean, who used a hand cycle bike and wheelchair to complete the race in 1997. Wills of iron, indeed.

Swimming, running, and biking what most people would consider masochistic distances in a single day—for fun—is a relatively recent phenomenon, but athletic individuals committed to mastering multiple disciplines have existed for centuries. Like the cavaliers of late medieval Europe. To earn the moniker, these robust soldiers had to have maximum proficiency in the three most important facets of knighthood: horsemanship, arms, and chivalry. There's also a trifecta of talents (i.e., flavors) in the Cavalier cocktail, a modern classic from bartender Sam Ross. This bright, herbaceous, less bitter Negroni offshoot, featuring gin, dry vermouth, and Amaro Montenegro, is a testament to the diverse and divergent skills necessary to make both a successful triathlete and a complex, well-balanced drink.

When it comes to having a few drinks after a competition, professional triathletes, like most of their peers, are a mixed bag—some partake and some don't. But a recent study shows that serious recreational endurance athletes, on average, take the mantra "earn your beers" to heart, drinking significantly more than their sedentary counterparts.

Recipe follows

CAVALIER

MAKES 1 DRINK

1 ounce London dry gin, such as Beefeater
1 ounce dry vermouth
1 ounce Amaro Montenegro
1 lemon twist, for garnish

Combine the gin, vermouth, and Amaro Montenegro in a double rocks glass. Add ice and stir with a long-handled spoon for 5 or 6 seconds. Rub the lemon twist around the rim of the glass, peel side down, then place it in the glass beside the ice.

AUSTRALIAN FOOTBALL LEAGUE GRAND FINAL

Saying the word "football," depending on where you are in the world, might result in some confusion as to which sport you're referring. In the Land Down Under, there's no such debate. Australian-rules football, inspired by the same English public-school games that spawned soccer and rugby, is that country's most popular spectator sport—by far. Massive crowds regularly come to Australian Football League (AFL) games to watch the best players in dynamic, high-jumping, high-kicking, full-contact action. But nothing comes close to the atmosphere of the league's annual season-ending match, the AFL Grand Final. It's usually the planet's most-attended domestic league championship event, hosting more than 100,000 ultra-boisterous fans who pack the Melbourne Cricket Ground for both the game and the lavish postgame festivities that include the winning team hoisting the AFL's premiership flag and receiving the league's cup and gold medallions. In recent decades, that infectious enthusiasm has begun to make its way around the globe, with amateur Aussie rules leagues springing up in far-flung places like Japan, Croatia, and French Guiana. This adds further perplexity when someone brings up football, while introducing millions to an exciting and highly watchable sport.

Aussie-rules football isn't the only piece of Australian culture making waves outside its homeland. Recently, the country's spirits industry has exploded, with highly regarded Australian wines, gins, rums, and whiskeys available pretty much everywhere booze is sold. Producers have even delved into the world of vermouth, with companies like Regal Rogue creating some delightful fortified wines with local ingredients like lemon myrtle and desert lime. Their Lively White vermouth, alongside limoncello, forms the base of the Lively Australian, a charming, zesty, and fizzy refresher that's ideal both as a post-match tipple or when you just want to soak up the action.

Aussie-rules football and booze have been intertwined since the sport's earliest days in the mid-nineteenth century. Opposing clubs would often share a pre-match champagne lunch, during which players and managers would strategically attempt to ply their rivals with free beverages. The team that won the contest was often the one that was the least inebriated. After the match, drinking resumed.

LIVELY AUSTRALIAN

MAKES 1 DRINK

1½ ounces semi-dry white vermouth, such as Regal Rogue Lively White Vermouth
1½ ounces limoncello
Club soda, to top
1 leaf fresh basil, for garnish
1 grapefruit slice, for garnish

Combine the vermouth and limoncello in a shaker. Add 1 or 2 ice pebbles, shake for 5 seconds, and pour into an ice-filled Collins glass. Top with club soda. Place the basil leaf in the glass beside the ice and perch the grapefruit slice on the rim of the glass.

CRICKET WORLD CUP

Despite what baseball obsessives might believe, in much of the world, the word "batter" refers to those of the cricket variety. The grandfather of modern bat-and-ball games, a recognizable version of cricket was being played in England as early as the mid-1500s, spreading worldwide as the British Empire expanded. While the first verified international match took place in 1844—a contest, oddly, between clubs from the U.S. and Canada in Manhattan—it wasn't until 1975 that the International Cricket Council organized the first Cricket World Cup, the sport's major international championship, a quadrennial face-off that's considered the pinnacle of the global cricket calendar. Since the first tournament, a victory for the West Indies team, the Cup has been hosted by nations on five continents, including Australia, which won six of the first thirteen finals. Wherever it's held, massive crowds and millions of TV viewers are guaranteed hours of extraordinary play and an energy that's palpable, even if, like most Americans, you may not understand exactly what's happening.

For many top cricketers, triumphantly hoisting the elusive ICC Cricket World Cup Trophy is the ultimate career goal. The focal point of the award is a large gold sphere, representative of a cricket ball, with its seam tilted to represent the axial tilt of the Earth. That well-known projectile (the ball, not the planet) and its distinctive red color also serve as inspiration for the Cricket Ball, a divinely fizzy and complex cocktail from the Red Cat, a Manhattan lounge located minutes from the site of the 1844 match. First appearing in print in Brad Thomas Parsons's *Bitters* (2011), this prosecco-packed party in a glass features bold notes of aperitif Lillet Rouge and two kinds of bitters, for a multilayered sip that's worthy of both cricket superstars and the world's most discerning bubbly enjoyers.

Beer and champagne have been so synonymous with cricket wins that fans were shocked during the 2023 World Cup, when the notoriously hard-partying Australian national team was photographed in their locker room celebrating a championship victory without so much as a bottle. That's because the match was held in Ahmedabad, India, where the manufacturing, sale, and public consumption of alcohol are banned. According to some later Instagram posts, however, the Aussies were able to partake in plenty of traditional celebratory activities in the privacy of their hotel rooms.

CRICKET BALL

MAKES 1 DRINK

1 white sugar cube
3 dashes Peychaud's bitters
3 dashes rhubarb bitters, such as Fee Brothers Rhubarb Bitters
1 ounce Lillet Rouge
Prosecco, to top
1 lemon twist, for garnish

Drop the sugar cube into the bottom of a champagne flute or coupe and douse the cube with both bitters. Add the Lillet Rouge. Top with prosecco and stir until the sugar cube dissolves. Rub the lemon twist around the rim of the glass, peel side down, then perch it on the rim of the glass.

NATHAN'S HOT DOG EATING CONTEST

Fancy a hot dog? How about seventy-six? That's the number of frankfurters (and corresponding buns) consumed in ten minutes by competitive eating icon Joey Chestnut at the 2021 edition of Coney Island, Brooklyn's Nathan's Hot Dog Eating Contest. Which, as of this writing, is still the world record. Chestnut's extraordinary gluttony, as well as his storied rivalry with six-time champion Takeru "The Tsunami" Kobayashi and the introduction of a women's division, helped the event achieve unprecedented popularity in the mid-2000s, cementing its status as the preeminent competitive eating competition. A far cry from its early days in the 1960s and 1970s as a minor publicity stunt for wiener purveyors Nathan's Famous, Inc., the contest regularly attracts upwards of 40,000 spectators and millions more around the world who watch it live on ESPN and place bets on their favorite Major League Eating (MLE) superstars gunning for the coveted bejeweled mustard-yellow belt. Hot dogs and high drama, who'da thunk it?

Due to their prevalence at sporting events, hot dogs are commonly associated with light domestic beer, but according to the *Drink & Pair* blog, America's favorite fleshy tubes of processed meat also go great with more complex, grape-based beverages: "The best wines to pair with hot dogs are Beaujolais, Zinfandel, Riesling, and Pinot Grigio, as all four are versatile, acidic (to some degree), and relatively inexpensive."

Anyone who's spent time at ballparks, basketball courts, or hockey rinks (or concerts, beaches, cookouts, etc., etc.) can attest to the symbiotic relationship between a hot dog and an ice-cold beverage. But combining the two in one wiener-licious, sippable package? It might sound like madness, yet frankfurter fanatic Randy Hansen has done just that with his Frank Collins, a savory and surprisingly palatable bit of ingenuity that starts with boiling hot dogs in water to create what Hansen calls "frank consommé," which serves as the drink's flavorful backbone. Embellished with gin, beer, Worcestershire sauce, and hot sauce, the Bloody Mary or Bullshot-esque end result is as adventurous as a career in competitive eating. And the best part, if your taste buds aren't already on weenie overload, is you've got some freshly cooked dogs to feast on while you sip it.

Recipe follows

FRANK COLLINS

MAKES 1 DRINK

1½ ounces gin
1½ ounces Frank Consommé (recipe follows)
4 dashes Worcestershire sauce
2 dashes hot sauce, such as Cholula
¼ ounce fresh lemon juice
Light beer, preferably an American lager, to top
1 fully cooked hot dog, hot or cold, for garnish

Combine the gin, frank consommé, Worcestershire sauce, hot sauce, and lemon juice in a shaker. Add 1 or 2 ice pebbles, shake for 5 seconds, and pour into an ice-filled Collins glass. Top with beer. Place the hot dog in the glass beside the ice.

Frank Consommé

MAKES APPROXIMATELY 28 OUNCES

4 cups water
4 to 6 hot dogs

Pour the water into a large saucepan and bring to a boil. Add the hot dogs, return the water to a boil, and cook for 5 to 7 minutes. Transfer the hot dogs to a plate to cool. Use immediately.

WORLD TABLE TENNIS CHAMPIONSHIPS

If you've ever gotten uncharacteristically heated, nay, borderline violent, over the disputed results of a basement or barroom table tennis match that started out amicably, you know how quickly the game can go from fun to infuriating. Only the coolest heads—and fastest reflexes—prevail at the World Table Tennis Championships, the premier biennial gathering of the planet's top-ranked paddlers, a thrilling display of agility and mental toughness that was first held in England—the sport's origin country—in 1926. Quickly spreading around the world, Ping-Pong (as it was popularly known) came to be dominated by the Hungarians, Japanese, and finally the Chinese, who own the most gold medals and remain the most formidable power in the game today. Regardless of where they're from, intelligent players all understand one thing: that, just as with guests at any respectable man cave or she shed table, a tantrum will do nothing but get you sent home, fast.

In its early, Victorian-era days as after-dinner parlor entertainment, table tennis was played exclusively by the British upper classes and was called whiff-waff. The words "ping pong" first appeared in the title of a song that was performed on London stages, and it wasn't until 1901, around the time when James Gibb invented the first bouncy, celluloid ball, that the sport and the phrase became synonymous. It's uncertain whether the Ping Pong cocktail—which first appeared in the 1930 Harry Craddock classic, *Savoy Cocktail Book*, but is probably much older—derived its name from the song or the sport. But this rich and floral after-dinner delicacy deftly recalls table tennis's aristocratic origins. And the quick-to-fix combo of sloe gin, violet flower, and citrus makes for a great semisweet treat to celebrate a match-winning kill shot or a consolation prize when the paddles don't swing your way.

On college campuses, the most popular Ping-Pong spin-off game is undoubtedly beer pong, which, according to the *Foodbeast* blog, started at Dartmouth University in the late 1950s, when fraternity brothers playing Ping-Pong noticed that their beer cups resting on the table could become targets. While the earliest versions of the game required handleless Ping-Pong paddles to hit balls into an opponent's cup, by the 1980s, beer pong—also known as "Beirut"—had evolved into the version with which most people are familiar today, in which players simply throw Ping-Pong balls into their opponents' geometrically arranged cups, forcing them to drink after each successful attempt.

Recipe follows

PING PONG

MAKES 1 DRINK

1 ounce sloe gin
1 ounce crème de violette
¾ ounce fresh lemon juice
1 lemon twist, for garnish

Combine the sloe gin, crème de violette, and lemon juice in an ice-filled shaker. Shake vigorously for 15 seconds and strain into a coupe. Rub the lemon twist around the rim of the glass, peel side down, then place it in the glass.

THE IDITAROD

Planning an early-March Alaskan excursion? Perhaps you'd be interested in eight to fifteen days on a hazardous dog sled, traveling more than 900 miles across sketchy terrain at breakneck speed through frequent blizzards, whiteout conditions, and gale-force winds that cause temperatures to drop as low as negative 100 degrees Fahrenheit, all while managing the whims and appetites of a dozen or more high-strung canine companions. Sound like fun?

For Alaska's professional sled-dog racers, or mushers, there's nothing better than the Iditarod Trail Sled Dog Race (or simply, the Iditarod), an annual test of endurance that pits the sport's toughest men and women against one another—and the elements—as they traverse the mostly wild tundra from Anchorage to Nome. Established in 1974, the Iditarod is not only the state's biggest sporting event but also a celebration and reminder of an 8,000-year way of life that's been mostly replaced by modern forms of transportation.

Although some mushers prefer to camp at random places along the trail, there are twenty-seven official checkpoints where they can rest, re-up on gear and supplies, and enjoy a hearty meal for themselves and their dogs after a tough day in the wilderness. If you're looking for Arctic-inspired refreshment from the much more comfortable confines of your home bar, try the Kodiak Sled Dog. This slightly more complex White Russian variation, featuring delectable notes of vanilla, chocolate, hazelnut, and coffee, packs a ton of flavor—and calories—into its creamy and silky confines. But when you're trying to survive the winter, there's nothing wrong with being a little husky (which, coincidentally, is today's preferred sled dog breed).

For Alaskans, who live in a state where major professional sports are nonexistent, the Iditarod is akin to the Super Bowl in terms of popularity. Nowhere is this more evident than during the days leading up to the race's ceremonial start in downtown Anchorage, where a carnival atmosphere called the Fur Rendezvous ("Fur Rondy," to the locals) takes over, featuring Ferris wheels and roller coasters, an ice sculpture contest, a "running of the reindeer" event, and a blanket toss—an ancient tradition of Alaskan natives. A few miles outside of town, along the mushers' opening trail, thousands of rowdy revelers enjoy "trailgate" parties, where DJs, stiff drinks, wild fashion, and dancing in sub-frigid temperatures are the order of the day.

KODIAK SLED DOG

MAKES 1 DRINK

1 ounce Canadian whisky
1 ounce Bailey's Irish Cream
1 ounce Frangelico hazelnut liqueur
1 ounce coffee liqueur, preferably Kahlúa
2 or 3 splashes whole milk

Combine all ingredients in an ice-filled shaker. Shake vigorously for 15 seconds and strain over ice into a double rocks glass.

ACKNOWLEDGMENTS

Lots of gratitude is due to all the lovely folks who helped bring this book into the world, including my agent, Rica Allannic; the brilliant team at Union Square & Co., especially editors Caitlin Leffel and Nicole Fisher, editorial director Amanda Englander, and copyeditor Terry Deal; and Heedayah Lockman for the superb illustrations.

I'm sincerely indebted to the dozens of bartenders, living or long-gone, whose creations appear on these pages, as well as my coworkers at Little Branch who have made (almost) every night behind the bar feel like a privilege for nearly two (!) decades.

Much love to program director Kris Madejski and my fellow artists at the Fish Factory Creative Centre of Stöðvarfjörður, Iceland, where much of this book was written in blessed peace and quiet (blizzards and power outages notwithstanding).

And infinite thanks to my father, my greatest coach and biggest supporter, for not only instilling a lifelong passion for athletic fandom that borders on the maniacal, but also for showing me firsthand how sports provide us with the most powerful life lessons. This one's for you.

INDEX